Wild Palms
reader

Edited by **Roger Trilling**
and Stuart Swezey

Art Director **Yasushi Fujimoto**
Designer **Kayoko Suzuki + CAP**
DigiProd **Hard Werken**, Los Angeles

St. Martin's Press

D1088766

WHO WILL BUY THIS WONDERFUL MORNING? SUCH A SKY YOU NEVER DID SEE.

THE WILD PALMS READER

The material collected in this book was originally published, or is based on material written by Bruce Wagner, illustrated by Julian Allen and originally published, in DETAILS magazine.
Design by Yasushi Fujimoto
COVER photograph ©1990 Ana Barrado. All rights reserved.

Special thanks to: Janine Coughlin, Twisne Fan, Tony Krantz, Kaoru Matsuzaki, James Truman, and Bruce Wagner.

Page 78 is excerpted from an essay by Stephen A. Benton, MIT Media Laboratory, from the List Gallery Exhibition: *Synthetic Spaces: Holography at MIT, 1990* brochure. Page 79 is ©1992 Left Bank Books and Rebel Press. Page 84 is ©1990 Verso

PICTURE CREDITS:

p. 3: ©Ana Barrado. All rights reserved.
p. 4: Photo of David Warner: Bob D'Amico, all other photos by Craig Sjodin, ©1992 Capital Cities/ABC, Inc.
pp. 6-7: ©Ana Barrado. All rights reserved.
pp. 8-11: Photos by Ansel Adams, courtesy of the Library of Congress; "Lucky Cloud" by Kango Takamura
pp. 12-13: ©1983 Digital Productions. All rights reserved.
pp. 16-17: courtesy of the California Institute of Technology
pp. 28-29: page design by Robert Bergman-Unger
p. 40: ©1992 Capital Cities/ABC, Inc. Photo: Steven Granitz
p. 41: Photo: Lori Bush-Guiterrez
pp. 46-47: ©1992 Capital Cities/ABC, Inc. Photo: Craig Sjodin
p. 49: ©1992 Capital Cities/ABC, Inc. Photo: Bob D'Amico
p. 52: courtesy Dr. Arnold Scheibel, Brain Research Institute, UCLA
pp. 56-57: ©Robert Cameron's *Above Los Angeles*
p. 58: Photo: Robert Waldman
P. 59: Photo: Andrew Waisler
p. 64: "Bright Zashiki": Mizuno Katsuhiko, Angie Dickinson: ©1992 Capital Cities/ABC, Inc. Photo: Bob D'Amico
pp. 66-67: ©1992 Capital Cities/ABC, Inc. Photos: Bob D'Amico, ad design by Robert Bergman-Unger
pp. 68-69: Photo: James Chotas

p. 70: *Church at Domburg* ©Estate of P. Mondrian/ E.M. Holtzman Trust, New York, New York
p. 71: Photo: Fredrik Nilsen
p. 73: courtesy Timex
pp. 74-75: courtesy Dr. Arnold Scheibel, Brain Research Institute, UCLA
pp. 80-81: Photos: Fredrik Nilsen, ad design by Robert Bergman-Unger
p. 84: Photo: James Chotas
p. 85: ©1992 Capital Cities/ABC, Inc. Photo: Sharon Beard
p. 86: ©1992 Capital Cities/ABC, Inc. Photo: Craig Sjodin
p. 93: courtesy Johns Hopkins Medical Institutions
pp. 96-97: from Max Ernst, *Maximiliana* ©1993 ARS, NY/SPADEM/ADAGP, Paris
p. 103: Go Chip Implanter designed by Doug Horlacker, Photo: Fredrik Nilsen
p. 106: courtesy Anglo-Australian Telescope Board
p. 107: *The Last Prince of Urbino* ©Joseph and Robert Cornell Memorial Foundation
pp. 110-111: Masafumi Sakamoto
p. 113: ©1992 Capital Cities/ABC, Inc. Photo: Craig Sjodin
p. 118: ©1992 Capital Cities/ABC, Inc. Photo: Craig Sjodin
pp. 120-121: courtesy Pacific Data Images
pp. 122-123: ©1987 Ana Barrado. All rights reserved.
pp. 124-125: center photo ©1992 Ana Barrado. All rights reserved.
p. 127: ©1992 Capital Cities/ABC, Inc. Photo: Sharon Beard

Photographs from Wild Palms courtesy of Capital Cities/ABC, Inc.
All WILD PALMS video images were taken by Glen Cannon.

First Edition: March 1993
10 9 8 7 6 5 4 3 2 1
Library of Congress Cataloging-in-Publication Data

The Wild palms reader / edited by Roger Trilling.
*** p. cm.
** "A Thomas Dunne book."
ISBN 0-312-09083-8
1. Wild palms (Television program) Trilling, Roger.
* PN1992.77.W47W5 1993
791.45'72——dc20 92-36317
CIP

Contents

All script excerpts were written by Bruce Wagner.
All excerpts from the WILD PALMS comic were written by Bruce Wagner, drawn by Julian Allen, and originally appeared in DETAILS magazine.
All of Anton Kreutzer's metaphysical writings were written by Genesis P. Orridge.

Anton Kreutzer — onetime science fiction writer turned visionary mystic; founder of Synthiotics a/k/a New Realism; co-founder of Mimecom

Corp.; started the Fathers to carry out policies; owner of Wild Palms Network; Senator and Presidential aspirant (Robert Loggia).

Josie Kreutzer-Ito — sister and only life-partner of Tony; married to Eli Levitt, then to Japanese industrialist Masahiro Ito;

Synthiotic empress of Japan and America (Angie Dickinson).

Eli Levitt — ex-professor of American History at Berkeley and Kyoto Universities; first husband of Josie; founder and leader of the Friends,

an organization dedicated to the overthrow of Kreutzer and the Fathers (David Warner).

Harry Wyckoff — putative son of Dex Wyckoff; married to Grace, patent lawyer and eventual head of Business Affairs at Wild Palms

Network (Jim Belushi).

Grace Wyckoff — daughter of Josie and Eli; married to Harry Wyckoff; mother of Coty and Deirdre (Dana Delany).

Chickie Levitt — son of Eli Levitt and his second wife; crippled by the Fathers; hardwire architect of the GO chip and "Einstein of

virtual reality" (Brad Dourif).

Paige Katz — daughter of Peter, muckraking anti-Fathers journalist who was murdered when she was three; brought up in a series

of Synthiotic foster homes; first love of Harry; longtime mistress of Tony (Kim Cattrall).

Coty Wyckoff — putative son of Grace and Harry; star of CHURCH WINDOWS, first holographic TV show; Synthiotic heir apparent (Ben Savage).

c a s t   o f
c h a r a c t e r

FADE IN:

CLOSE. HARRY WYCKOFF.
Harry at law office, talking on phone headset.

Harry (V.O.)
My name is Harry Wyckoff. I'm an attorney at Baum, Weiss and
Latimer. They promised to make me a partner, but somehow it never
happened; that made me feel weak. Still, the money's good.

CLOSE. GRACE WYCKOFF.
Stares directly into CAMERA; stands by rack of women's clothes.

Harry (V.O.)
My wife, Grace, is a designer. She owns a boutique on Melrose called
Vestiges. Lots of young celebrities shop there.

CLOSE. COTY WYCKOFF.
Turns to stare into CAMERA, in midst of playing video game.

Harry (V.O.)
Coty and I don't spend enough time together. He's already twelve. It's
practically a miracle to get to twelve without being molested.

CLOSE. DEIRDRE WYCKOFF.
Stares into CAMERA, smiling.

Harry (V.O.)
Deirdre smiles and stares and never cries. We call her Little Buddha.

CLOSE. HARRY.
In bed, beside sleeping wife. He stands, goes to window.

Harry (V.O.)
It started with a nightmare. I dreamed of black-and-blue skies choked
with stars; and palm trees rocked by wind. I dreamed a lot that year. . .

<u>Senator</u>
    We live in a desert — that's the world. We inherited it; no sense complaining. Some of us want to see it
<u>Harry</u>
    What?
<u>Senator</u>
    (swings at ball on tee; watches it arc)
    Not far from here, they found it: a lost city of children's imaginings.
<u>Harry</u>
    That drawing Paige gave me. I had some nightmares—
<u>Senator</u>
    (they begin to walk)
    You know what the rhino is, Harry? It's all that's left of the unicorn. A magnificent atavism — the
    exquisite. (laughs) You think I'm a tweaked old bastard, don't you?

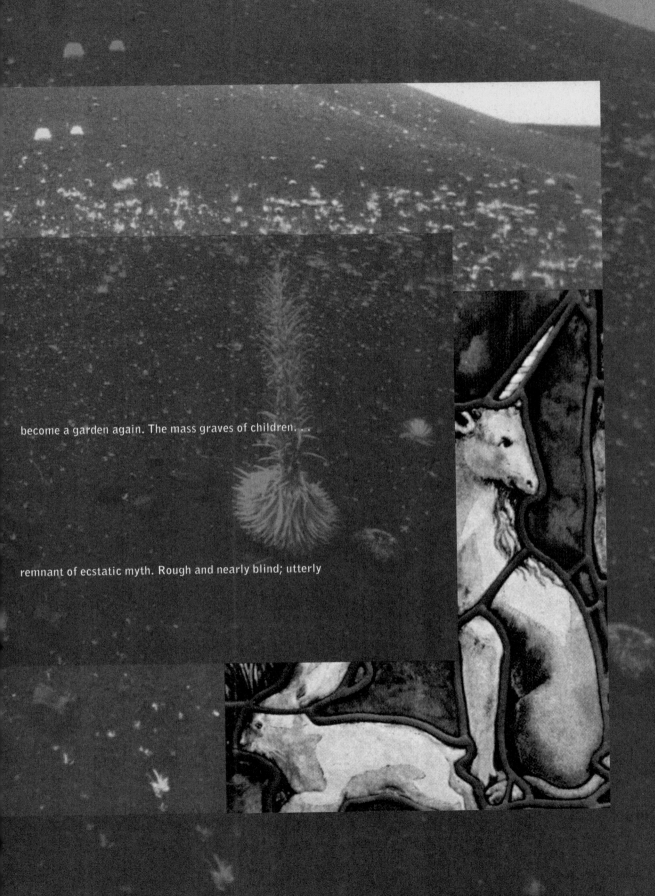

become a garden again. The mass graves of children. . .

remnant of ecstatic myth. Rough and nearly blind; utterly

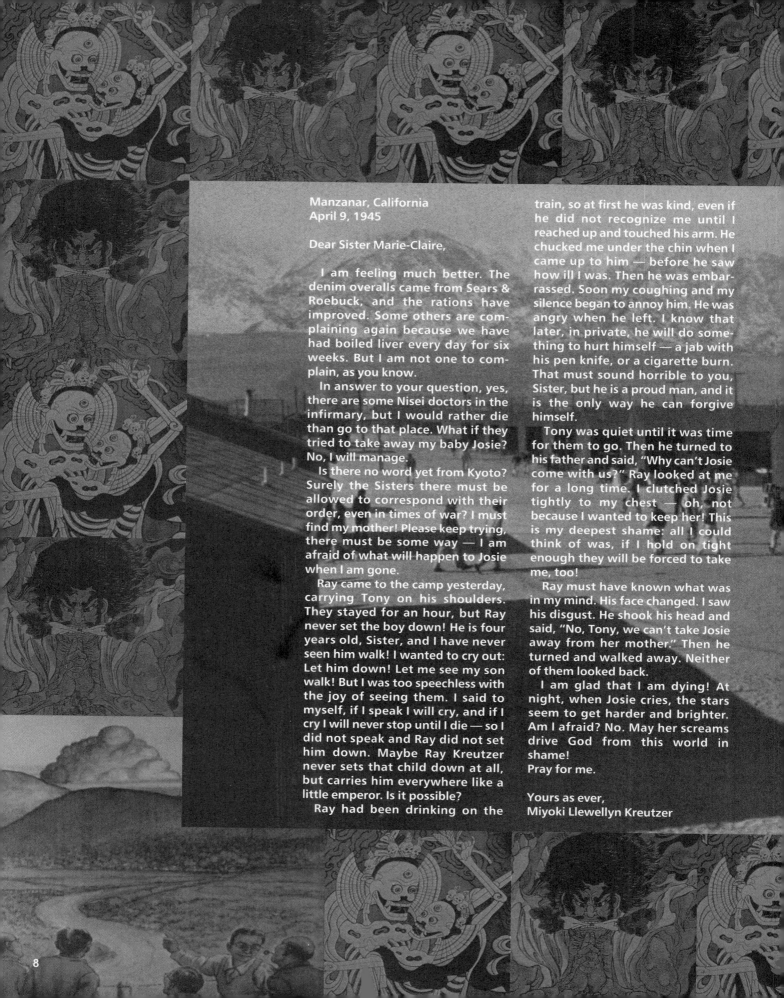

Manzanar, California
April 9, 1945

Dear Sister Marie-Claire,

I am feeling much better. The denim overalls came from Sears & Roebuck, and the rations have improved. Some others are complaining again because we have had boiled liver every day for six weeks. But I am not one to complain, as you know.

In answer to your question, yes, there are some Nisei doctors in the infirmary, but I would rather die than go to that place. What if they tried to take away my baby Josie? No, I will manage.

Is there no word yet from Kyoto? Surely the Sisters there must be allowed to correspond with their order, even in times of war? I must find my mother! Please keep trying, there must be some way — I am afraid of what will happen to Josie when I am gone.

Ray came to the camp yesterday, carrying Tony on his shoulders. They stayed for an hour, but Ray never set the boy down! He is four years old, Sister, and I have never seen him walk! I wanted to cry out: Let him down! Let me see my son walk! But I was too speechless with the joy of seeing them. I said to myself, if I speak I will cry, and if I cry I will never stop until I die — so I did not speak and Ray did not set him down. Maybe Ray Kreutzer never sets that child down at all, but carries him everywhere like a little emperor. Is it possible?

Ray had been drinking on the train, so at first he was kind, even if he did not recognize me until I reached up and touched his arm. He chucked me under the chin when I came up to him — before he saw how ill I was. Then he was embarrassed. Soon my coughing and my silence began to annoy him. He was angry when he left. I know that later, in private, he will do something to hurt himself — a jab with his pen knife, or a cigarette burn. That must sound horrible to you, Sister, but he is a proud man, and it is the only way he can forgive himself.

Tony was quiet until it was time for them to go. Then he turned to his father and said, "Why can't Josie come with us?" Ray looked at me for a long time. I clutched Josie tightly to my chest — oh, not because I wanted to keep her! This is my deepest shame: all I could think of was, if I hold on tight enough they will be forced to take me, too!

Ray must have known what was in my mind. His face changed. I saw his disgust. He shook his head and said, "No, Tony, we can't take Josie away from her mother." Then he turned and walked away. Neither of them looked back.

I am glad that I am dying! At night, when Josie cries, the stars seem to get harder and brighter. Am I afraid? No. May her screams drive God from this world in shame!
Pray for me.

Yours as ever,
Miyoki Llewellyn Kreutzer

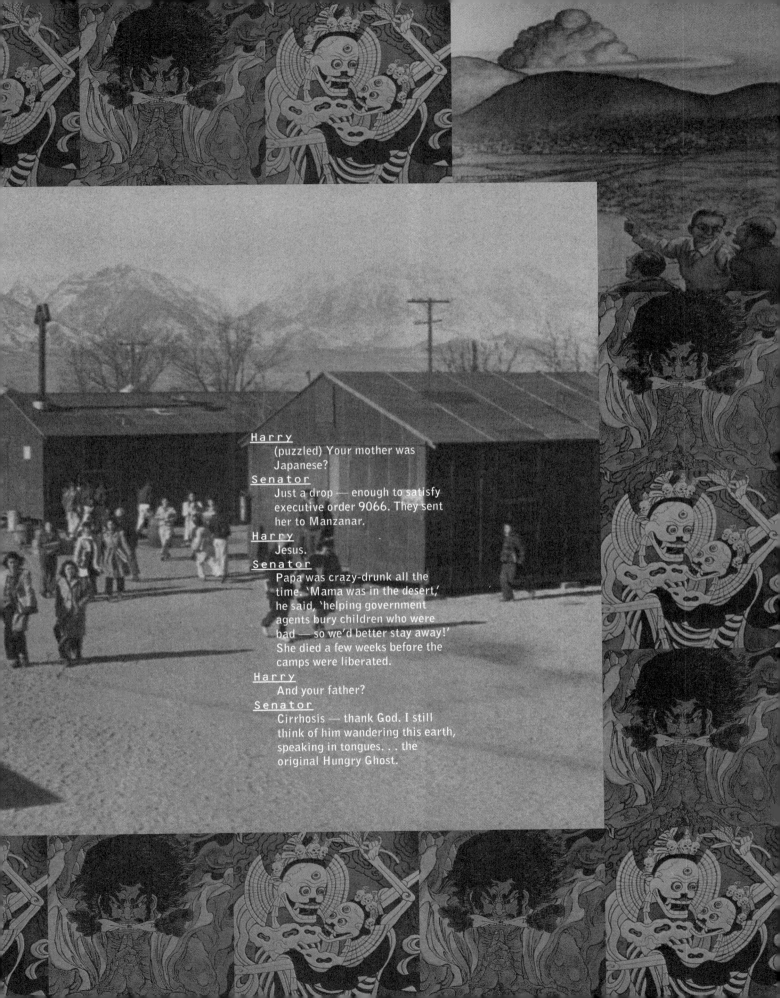

Harry
(puzzled) Your mother was
Japanese?

Senator
Just a drop — enough to satisfy
executive order 9066. They sent
her to Manzanar.

Harry
Jesus.

Senator
Papa was crazy-drunk all the
time. 'Mama was in the desert,'
he said, 'helping government
agents bury children who were
bad — so we'd better stay away!'
She died a few weeks before the
camps were liberated.

Harry
And your father?

Senator
Cirrhosis — thank God. I still
think of him wandering this earth,
speaking in tongues. . . the
original Hungry Ghost.

[All that's left of a story by Anton Kreutzer was found aboard The Floating World. Believed to be part of a book for children called *The Lost City*, it was composed by the Senator in the Fifties during stints in juvenile hall. We know from *Wild Psalms* that during these difficult years, the adolescent received great consolation from *Don Quixote*; Kreutzer too would write a manuscript while confined. This earliest of literary efforts now resides at the Research Library at UCLA, Special Collections.]

"But there are sandcastles in Catalina," Thomas protested.

"This is true," spoke Mr. Wilding, "but none can compare to those of Manzanar."

"But there is marlin and there is shark off the shores of Catalina," said Thomas. "Are there any fishes at Manzanar?"

"No," said Mr. Wilding. "There are no fishes at Manzanar."

So Thomas went with his mentor to Manzanar. They took Mr. Wilding's green Studebaker[1] onto the macadam highway. They had wicker baskets filled with fruit and potpourri and the sky above was like [a] molten [?] cathedral. "We're off to see the lizards," Mr. Wilding sang, and Thomas joined him, laughing. "The wonderful lizards of Oz . . ."

* * *

[. . .] a hundred trucks. There were families sitting in their cars, waiting. The sound of birds came from the dank restrooms.

Thomas watched them carry the boy into a Quonset hut made of cinderblocks. Mr. Wilding was solemn as he worked; [he] rubbed him awhile and the boy was cured.[2]

* * *

"[. . .] lost city of children's imaginings."

Thomas looked around and was confused — he saw nothing but dunes. A lonely wind howled through the emptiness and the Studebaker clicked and growled, though Mr. Wilding had shut off its engine.

"I don't see anything," Thomas said.

"But you feel something, don't you?"

"I'm not sure."

Thomas stood outside himself a moment to see if he felt anything at all; he was only aware of the clicking car and a familiar smell in the air that he couldn't place.[3]

"Come," said Mr. Wilding. "I will bring you down."

They began to walk and as they did the air seemed to cool and the familiar smell became less so. Thomas trailed behind the tireless Mr. Wilding. Occasionally the boy looked back to see the Studebaker recede. He was glad not to hear the automobile's lonely noises yet there was something disturbing about its diminution.

"There's Simon!"[4] shouted Mr. Wilding.

Thomas squinted ahead but saw nothing.

"I don't see anyone."

"There!" Mr. Wilding was pointing furiously while he jumped. "On the pillar."

Thomas gasped — there before him was a boy with green hair.[5] He stood on a pillar like a model in a store window; the pillar revolved so that Thomas had to walk around it counterclockwise in order to watch the Boy's face. Mr. Wilding threw his head back and laughed.

"Hey, you! You with the corruscated heart!" bellowed the Boy.

Mr. Wilding convulsed with laughter; Thomas stood suddenly frozen. The pillar revolved and the Boy strained his head this way and that so his eyes never left the new arrival.

"Simon, this is Thomas."

＊ ＊ ＊

"Well, I suppose it's all right," said the Boy to Mr. Wilding. "All the same, I hope you told him."

Thomas turned to his mentor, who was smiling still.

"'Told him' — what does he mean?"

"That you are leaving this world, never to come back."

The pillar had by now lowered itself to ground level. Mr. Wilding seized Thomas by the hand and walked him over. The boy with green hair stepped to the edge; the pillar's top was more spacious than Thomas imagined. It felt good being close to the Boy. As they descended beneath the dunes, Thomas caught sight once more of the abandoned Studebaker. He felt an unearthly, unbearable nostalgia and his body shook with exhaustion that sprang from some nameless, thoughtless place. He was embarrassed, standing outside himself again,[6] watching his body shake. Mr. Wilding was unaware of Thomas' travails; he stared off into nothingness, as if he was dead.

"I'm sorry," Thomas said to the Boy as darkness enveloped them. He said it again, then over and over — other words wouldn't come.

The Boy reached over and held Thomas close. "They call that the 'tremendum,'" he said, with great tenderness. "Happens to everyone. The Studebaker is heavy for you, dense like a dead star; it's all you'll remember of the place you called home. That car made itself a gift to you, a gift of the gone world. You'll learn to cherish that silly Studebaker like it was the saddest, most beautiful poem that ever was. Which, of course, it is."

Thomas felt a great weight lift from him; then there was the sound of a thousand children's voices reaching up like a carnival of caressing hands. Indeed, it *was* a lost city. He held onto the Boy as they dropped from the vertiginous dome of the desert to the waiting throng. Their sweet, painted faces floated up —

1. The same car Kreutzer's father drove from the Panhandle to Angel's Flight, in the '30's.

2. Over the years, this cryptic section has elicited a host of theories. From *King of Kings* by Macall Polay (Random House, 2009): "The broken family began many trips to visit Mama at Manzanar; Anton's spirits would soar as the place came into view, only to be dashed when Ray roared past the gates and back onto the highway, laughing maniacally. He was severely deviated; highway rest stops would have given him an opportunity to cathect on his helpless son. In *The Lost City*, that son bravely, poignantly transforms a desecration of his body by the ultimate Father into a great healing."

3. "The rancorous, animal smell of a father's anus." (Polay)

4. Ironically, *Simon of the Desert* was to become one of Kreutzer's most beloved films. Bunuel remained a favorite throughout the Senator's lifetime; his complete filmography is available (holodisc) in the Synthiotics catalogue.

5. Another of Kreutzer's favorites was *The Boy With Green Hair* (RKO, 1948). Dean Stockwell was to become a prominent New Realist; he is still an active fundraiser.

6. A recurrent description among victims of child sexual abuse.

THE APOTHEOSIS
Richard

from *The Cathedral at the End of Time* (1963)

— Anton Kreutzer

Chapter the Last:
The Apotheosis of Richard Philo

The Cathedral awaited him.

It stood complete now, rising above the radioactive ruins of what had been, for a few short magnificent years, the city that seemed to be what it had all been leading up to, the final ripened fruit of Western Civilization — Los Angeles, City of Angels, Factory of Dreams. Then the bombs had fallen, and the City of Angels had become Death's vastest, most expensive ruin. Skyscrapers disintegrated in atomic winds. Beaches fused to glass. Where captive waters had nourished gardens to rival Babylon's, the desert had resumed its ancient tyranny. Scorpions and lizards were the only heirs of man.

But he had changed that. He'd dug down into the ashes of the pit and grasped the jewel wrought by the apocalypse, and he had built the setting for the jewel, and it was mounted there now, the transub-stantiated host that pulsed at the heart of the Cathedral, a single matte black wafer of lusterless glass no bigger than one of the stones on a Go gameboard.

Yet containing an unimaginable power.

And now, after all the years of struggle against those who had doubted and derided his vision, against the others who'd believed him but wanted to pervert his vision to their venal ends, against his own insane father, at last that power was to be focused and channeled through him. And then, by passing through him, it would flow forth through all humankind, the redeeming blood of a post-Apocalyptic Christ.

He stepped up to the podium that had been built before the vast portal of the Cathedral. The crowd assembled before him fell silent. They did not cheer or chant his name, as they had at earlier ceremonies, for they shared his awe at the solemnity of the moment.

The culmination of human history. Here compressed into a single slim cone of glass was the spiritual and mental essence of the Pyramids

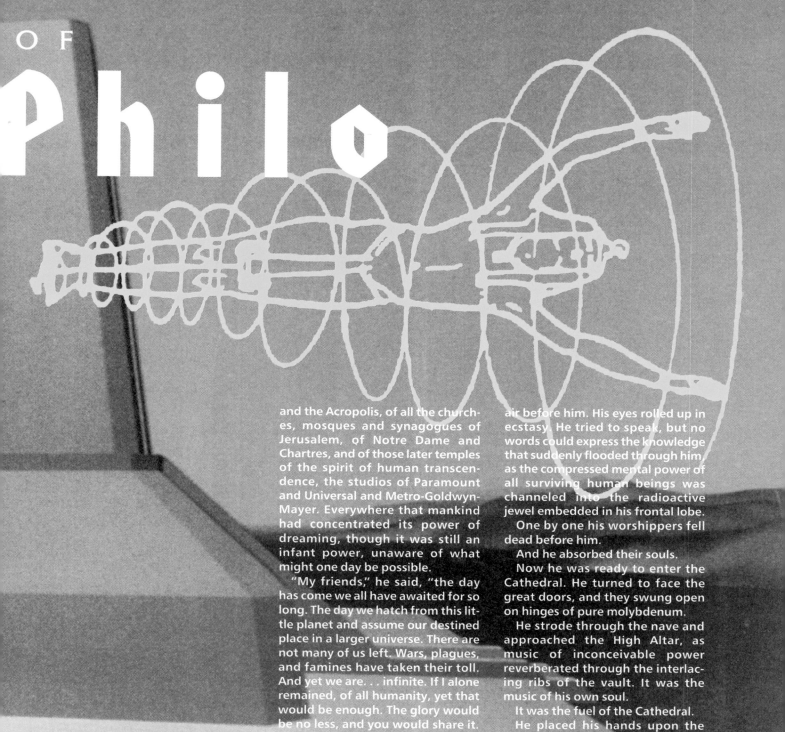

and the Acropolis, of all the churches, mosques and synagogues of Jerusalem, of Notre Dame and Chartres, and of those later temples of the spirit of human transcendence, the studios of Paramount and Universal and Metro-Goldwyn-Mayer. Everywhere that mankind had concentrated its power of dreaming, though it was still an infant power, unaware of what might one day be possible.

"My friends," he said, "the day has come we all have awaited for so long. The day we hatch from this little planet and assume our destined place in a larger universe. There are not many of us left. Wars, plagues, and famines have taken their toll. And yet we are. . . infinite. If I alone remained, of all humanity, yet that would be enough. The glory would be no less, and you would share it. You *will* share it.

"Now!"

He bowed his head to receive the diadem of his transmutation.

The technicians aimed the beam of the super-acceletron at the forehead of Richard Philo, and a slim cone of crimson light, like the horn of a unicorn, seemed to form in the air before him. His eyes rolled up in ecstasy. He tried to speak, but no words could express the knowledge that suddenly flooded through him, as the compressed mental power of all surviving human beings was channeled into the radioactive jewel embedded in his frontal lobe.

One by one his worshippers fell dead before him.

And he absorbed their souls.

Now he was ready to enter the Cathedral. He turned to face the great doors, and they swung open on hinges of pure molybdenum.

He strode through the nave and approached the High Altar, as music of inconceivable power reverberated through the interlacing ribs of the vault. It was the music of his own soul.

It was the fuel of the Cathedral.

He placed his hands upon the Altar, and the floor trembled beneath him as the Cathedral lifted off and rose, rocket-like, into the metaverse that was, at once, himself and all humanity and infinite space and eternal time.

And he became. . . Creator God.

The End. . . of the Beginning

'Let me go.' Everybody wants to go — especially Senator
Kreutzer. He is the Go-Master. . . And Josie's the go-go girl!

US Consulate
Division of Cultural Affairs
Kyoto, Japan
August 28, 1967

Dear Tony,

I saw your short story, "Pyramid Scheme," in As-imov's magazine. The consulate librarian ordered a subscription when I told her my brother was a regular contributor. We lowly clerks have our perks too!

This one is my favorite of all your stories. I like the idea of "God" as a race of aliens who create mankind in order to use human "faith" as fuel to project them-selves through time and space — thus becoming immortal. God creates man and man creates God, ad infinitum.

You may not know it, but this is close to the Japanese philosophy of Go. Go teaches that all events have con-sequences that permeate all other events. It's a kind of multi-dimensional karma. Through Go, the past, pre-sent and future are one. The "fuel" of men and gods is called *tama*. Life-force would be a bad translation of it — your story gets the idea much better. It is a precious substance, even though it inhabits everything — rocks, plants, animals and man.

There are some very dangerous Shinto rituals that are said to bind *tama* to the personality rather than the body — immortality, in a nutshell. Still, all of these paths to immortality somehow include death as a matter of course. Sounds suspicious. But most people in Japan are more concerned with hanging onto the *tama* they've got. Many Japanese tie a knot in one sleeve to keep their *tama* from escaping. Not me.

Your story reminded me of a time I had long forgot-ten, when father used to tie us to the bed each night as he tucked us in. Didn't he used to say that this was because we were so beautiful the angels might steal us from him in the night? Later, every time he burst into the darkened room in a drunken rage, I dreamed that you and I would leave our bodies and float into the air, holding hands. I would look down on our lifeless arms and legs, his sweating naked body bearing down on one or the other of us, and I would feel a soft, buoyant ecstasy. The pain was so intense that it liberated me. I have not since found a way to repeat the experience — now that father is dead, I may be trapped in my body forever. Did you have the same dream, Tony? Isn't that a little like what the stranded God does in your story, when he gets a jump-start into eternity from the ancient Egyptians? I traveled up to the ceiling on the strength of my own suffering. Who knows — if one could gather the *tama* of a billion souls, how long and how far might one Go?

I can send you some books on Shinto religious cults if you like. Maybe they would give you some ideas.

Love,
Josie

What does the man of renunciation do? He strives for a higher world, he wants to fly further and higher than all men of affirmation — he throws away much that would encumber his flight, including not a little that he esteems and likes; he sacrifices it to his desire for the heights. This sacrificing, this throwing away, however, is precisely what alone becomes visible and leads people to call him the man of renunciation: it as such that he confronts us, shrouded in his hood, as if he were the soul of a hairshirt. But he is quite satisfied with the impression he makes on us: he wants to conceal from us his desire, his pride, his intention to soar beyond us. Yes, he is cleverer than we thought and so polite to us — this man of affirmation. For that is what he is, no less than we, even in his renunciation.

. . . We can no longer conceal from ourselves what exactly it is that this whole process of willing, inspired by the ascetic ideal, signifies — this hatred of humanity, of animality, of inert matter; this loathing of the senses, of reason even; this fear of beauty and happiness; this longing to escape from illusion, change, becoming, death, and from longing itself. It signifies, let us have the courage to face it, a will to nothingness, a revulsion from life, a rebellion against the principal conditions of living. And yet, despite everything, it is and remains a will. Let me repeat, now that I have reached the end, what I said at the beginning: man would sooner have the void for his purpose than be void of purpose. . . .

— Friedrich Nietzsche

There is a time that each of us knows that comes without warning. Suddenly it comes and so silently, and it descends upon us like a net, a grid of light. Indifferent to our plans or our hour it falls on us, and however our time was allotted and conceived the plan fades away under that light as though the lines were lead in church windows. In the final furnace of transmutation, no fact remains, all hallucinations are equal.

In that light we begin to see, not with the eyes of our mind; but with an eye behind our mind we begin to finally see, to shed nature's trap, the physical body, the bondage of compassion.

And in that light these things are heard and seen, but they are seen not from without but from within. From a place deep within a map of stars where there is no distinction of words or of actions but only a discernment of feeling and in that LIGHT it is not feeling that is regarded, because all that is done with feeling melts and dissolves like sand into glass. What must be regarded is the Lack of All Feeling. For feeling is shallow, and thin, and so, so empty, a hungry worthless ghost.

Faces come before you, and expressions, and you see all of the face is held together only for expression, for an idea, and you watch the face before you and there is nothing else besides, and the mouth moves, opens, and smiles and the eyes look at you and sometimes they are saying what the mouth is saying and sometimes they aren't saying that, but something else, or nothing, or anything and no answer but a lie comes.

The idea rides on words but is the distant watcher, the substance of eternity. It is the invisible warrior astride the pale unicorn deep in space, waiting for the brave and hungry.

The *kamagikushi* gives silence to the wordless. The sound that is all around you is the sound of a hundred liars.

— Anton Kreutzer, *Garden of Infinity (1967)*

Harry

That's who you work for? The guy who founded that religion in the sixties?

Paige

Synthiotics. It's helped a lot of people.

Harry

'New Realism.' Very hip now. Read about it in **People**. . .

Paige

Don't be so cynical. You should read some of his books.

Harry

I don't dig bad science fiction.

THE BIRTH OF **MIME·COM**

TONY KREUTZER, I'VE READ "GARDEN OF INFINITY" IT SEEMS YOU'VE FOUND A DOOR

AND I HEAR YOU HAVE THE KEY TO OPEN IT, DEX

'92 SPAIN

1969 AT A COMMUNE IN SEBASTOPOL

THIS IS MY OLD LADY, BERNICE U##ER I MEAN, MARAKESH

DEX TEACHES TONY TO PLAY GO

I HEAR YOU'VE BEEN CHECKING OUT FUGU

A SMALL AMOUNT OF WHAT WOULD OTHERWIZE KILL YOU WILL TRANSPORT YOU TO OTHER REALMS

BUT I'M WORKING ON SOME CIRCUITS THAT WILL REALLY PUT YOU "UP ON THE MOUNTAIN"

THIS IS IT MAN, NO DRUGS, NO CHEMICALS. ONCE I GET THIS SET UP, JUST **ZOOM!** INTO THE NEXT DIMENSION

DEX IS SO UPTIGHT LATELY

YOU GOTTA GIVE HIM SOME SPACE. HE'S GOT A LOT ON HIS MIND THESE DAYS

HUNT DETECTIVE AGENCY
138 FOLSOM STREET
SAN FRANCISCO, CALIFORNIA

CLIENT: A. KREUTZER

SUBJ.: TRANSCRIPT OF TELEPHONE
CONVERSATION BETWEEN "DEX"
WYCKOFF AND PETER SIMON
(SIMON AND SIMON
MANAGEMENT CONSULTANTS),
JANUARY 21, 1971

D W : It's Dex.

P S : Yeah?

D W : I got some more ideas on the prospectus.

P S : Dex, I'm working my ass off. Would you just leave it?

D W : Listen, I know you've been trying to stay away from Tony's stuff because it spooks the money people, but you're blowing the main point, man. The way to buffer the Synthiotics thing isn't to bury it. Just, I don't know, tone it down —

P S : Look, Dex, we're having enough trouble calming them down about your blotter business, and Tony's trip just scares the shit out of them. You heard that stuff Englebart's buddy was saying. Christ, Earhart blew up their lab! They got guys wandering the mountains with comic books —

D W : That won't happen here! Do you see any of that kind of confusion around here? Synth may be a heavy rap, but the philosophy — this isn't some weird cult, Pete! You —

P S : Tell it to ABC! Christ —

D W : Pete — Pete, listen to me. We're talking about MENTAL AUGMENTATION. You know what that means? We can link brains with computers. We can expand consciousness so much that a human being can take in all the information in the fucking universe and see RELATIONSHIPS. Hell, we don't know what wisdom means yet! But we know how to find out! It's like a two-way membrane, your wisdom becoming part of a vast collective wisdom that will live forever — I know it's so big it's scary, but man, you gotta make the money guys see it. If they don't get it, how're we gonna get what we need? Do you understand how big this is?

P S : Yeah, Dex, I understand what YOU think —

D W : We're talking about human evolution here! The end of the whole fucked up history of the world!

P S : Do you hear yourself, Dex?

D W : Pete, okay. You just gotta tone it down. You gotta tone it down. Tony makes it scary, you gotta tone it down.

P S : Tony thinks he's Jesus Christ.

D W : Tony thinks about himself too much. Back off of it, man. Look, what did that Krishna kid say? The Pong kid? Empowerment, enlightenment — humans invented computers for enlightenment —

P S : Hippie shit. That kid's going nowhere!

D W : Okay, stop. People spend money to get happy, right?

P S : Shit.

D W : Listen, Pete. There's legal stuff, not scary stuff — there's precedents. Valium. Pong. So what if I told you I could make you a drug and a computer that would make you SMARTER, Pete? We don't have to talk about evolution with a capital E. Just talk about learning, learning aids. Things that make you better. And convince 'em we can do it. Can we show them any of the patent applications?

P S : Are you crazy?

D W : Gimme three more weeks and we'll have the demo done. We'll have your kid doing calculus, man —

P S : Leave my kid out of it. Dex, even if I could convince them, the education stuff just won't sell. These guys want to make money. GAMES are gonna make money, not marijuana flashcards —

D W : (laughter) Tell it to the FDA! They got a FINE record on recreational drugs —

P S : — and it's not going to be ENOUGH money —

D W : Look, I told you before, we develop the heavy metal for the space program and get the government to pay for the research. We can make the 1802 look like a stone axe, man! Talk to that guy Craig again. Christ, those guys are hemorrhaging money! And we build some consumer stuff to bring in more bucks — more bucks than these guys have ever seen! And between the two we have enough money to pay for our own R&D, and we don't have to tell anybody about that until we're ready to change the water.

P S : Okay, Dex, okay. I'll work on it. I'll get you something tomorrow maybe.

D W : We okay, man?

P S : We're okay.

###END###

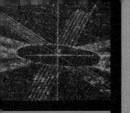

AY DON'T WORRY ABOUT IT! YOU COME UP WITH THE BUCKS AND I GUARANTEE THE PATENTS

TONY I'M PREGNANT

THATS O.K. BABY. THE FUTURE, THAT'S WHAT WE'VE GOT TO THINK OF. WE'RE ON THE VERGE OF A COSMIC SOMERSAULT

DON'T GIVE ME THAT SHIT. YOU'RE THE ONE BRINGING THE "SUITS" AROUND HERE. THAT WASN'T OUR VISION ... AND DON'T THINK I DON'T KNOW WHAT'S GOING ON BEHIND MY BACK WITH BERENICE

DEX SUFFERS FROM A SELF INFLICTED GUN WOUND

IT'S UP TO US NOW TO CARRY ON DEX'S WORK. TOGETHER WE WILL DREAM THE WORLD UNTO THE ULTIMATE PLANE

AFTERWARD...

TODAY, GENTLEMEN, WE ARE ON THE VERGE OF TOMORROW. EVEN NOW OUR LABORATORIES ARE WORKING ON NEW CONCEPTS THAT WILL ...

MIMECOM CORPORATION

IEEE Transactions on Medical Electronics
v15 n3 July-September 1971, pp. 1175-1195

An Invasive Approach to High-Bandwidth
Neural-Electronic Interfaces

Dexter Wyckoff *principal scientist, Mimecom Seldon Research Center, Sebastopol, California*
Rajiv Kamar *research neurobiologist, Department of Psychology, University of California at San Francisco*
Fred Wright *computer systems engineer, Project One, Berkeley, California*

ABSTRACT In previous years one of the authors (Wyckoff) reported on the development of synthetic neurotransmitter analogs that, administered intravenously, enhanced certain mental functions, including memory formation and recall, and ability to maintain attention for extended periods. Further efforts in that direction yielded diminishing returns. In an offshoot of this work, the authors investigated the possibility of augmenting mental function by physically linking brain structures to external computer hardware. After locating a suitable neural connection site (the mammalian corpus callosum) we developed hardware and software for the task. This paper describes our first unambiguously successful results, obtained in a juvenile squirrel monkey, which was able, in consequence, to play chess and to read at the level of a schoolchild, activities far outside of its normal competence.

   Our approach generalizes straightforwardly to human augmentation, and points to the additional possibility of gradually migrating memories, skills and personality encoded in fragile and bounded neural hardware to faster, more capacious and communicative, and less mortal, external digital machinery — thus preserving and expanding the essential function of a mind, even as the nervous system in which it arose was lost. A mind and personality, as an information-bearing pattern, might thus be freed from the limitations and risks of a particular physical body to travel over information channels and reside in alternative physical hosts.

INTRODUCTION Traditionally, human central nervous systems (CNS) and electronic computation and communication devices have been linked via the bodily senses and musculature — an approach requiring only simple technology and incurring little medical risk. Unfortunately, this straightforward avenue has very low information bandwidth: effectively a few kilohertz of sensory information (primarily vision) into the CNS, and a mere one tenth of that figure out. Much higher transfer rates are observed within the CNS. In particular, the corpus callosum connects the right and left cerebral hemispheres with 500 million fibers in the human. Each fiber signals on average at about ten hertz, for an aggregate rate of several gigahertz: about one million times the bandwidth of the senses. The corpus callosum connects to all major cerebral areas, offering a spectacular opportunity for electronic interaction. The primary challenges are the invasive nature and massive scale of any comprehensive link. In other publications we have described the design of "neural combs" which can be inserted non-destructively into nerve bundles to make contact with a large fraction of the fibers: they are scaled up relatives of cochlear implants used in nerve-deafness surgery. This paper describes experiments in which neural combs were implanted into the callosa of primates, and connected to a computer running adaptive algorithms that modeled the measured neural traffic and correlated it with sensory, motor and cognitive states, and later impressed external information on this flow.

   The animals (squirrel monkeys) used in the experiments have a CNS size about one two-hundredth that of a human, with a corpus callosum of less than ten thousand fibers, greatly simplifying both the surgical and computational aspects of the work. In each experiment a neural comb with two thousand microfiber tines at ten micro separation, each carrying along its length one hundred separate connection rings, was carefully worked between the axons in the callosum of the experimental animal. After a week to heal surgical trauma, a cable bundle from the comb to a PDP-10 ten teraops multiprocessor was activated, and signals from the tines were processed by a factor-analysis program. Once a rough relational map had been obtained, a functional map was constructed by presenting the animal with controlled sensory stimuli, and inducing it to perform previously trained motor tasks, while correlating comb activity. The functional map was further refined by processing the responses to synthesized sensations introduced via the comb. After several days of stimulation and analysis, the PDP-10 had a sufficiently good model of the callosal traffic that we were able to elicit very complex and specific behaviors, including some that seem quite beyond the capacities of the unaugmented animals.

   Our most notable results were obtained with animal number three (#3), out of five subjects. In one demonstration, we interfaced #3 to the Greenblatt chess program, supplied with the PDP-10 software. We began by fast-training #3 to discriminate individual chess pieces we presented. Fast-training is similar to conventional operant conditioning, but greatly accelerated because

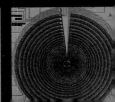

funding Future

September 22, 1973

To: The Director of the Department of Human Services, State of California

From: Tobias Schenkl, M. D. — Consulting Psychiatrist and Director of Clinical Trials for the Mimecom Corporation

Subject: Application for Funding of Street Rehabilitation Clinics

As a consulting psychiatrist under contract to the Mimecom Corporation of Sebastopol, California, I am writing to request a funding grant sufficient to support a one-year trial of five street clinics to be administered by the Corporation, beginning on January 1st of next year.

In the three months to date of our operational prototype, we have already come close to curing — permanently curing — of their self-destructive and anti-social behaviors: fifteen substance abusers; three compulsive gamblers; twenty paroled convicts (many of them repeat offenders); eight female and four male prostitutes. In addition, we have motivated twenty-three unemployed school dropouts to return to high school, and administered cost-free psychotherapy to thirteen young runaways who have now begun the effective healing of themselves and their dysfunctional parents.

The eighty-six people summarized above are drawn from the total of our eighty-nine clinical participants to date, while the remaining three alone have shown no demonstrable sign of improvement. In other words, our rate of success — success as measured by conventional psychometric indices of progress toward normalcy — is between ninety-six and ninety-seven percent.

These claims may appear slightly fantastic, I know. But we are able to document them with the attached testimonials from our subjects (full names and addresses available upon request), and with supporting letters from deans of the schools of social work throughout the University of California system. We invite you to contact them all.

How are we able to achieve such unprecedented, and such encouraging, results? Through three processes which, taken together, constitute an ensemble of mental technologies that we call Synthiotics.

Firstly, through *psychopharmacology*: through the (completely voluntary) ingestion of drugs under development by the Mimecom Corporation, which show dramatic promise of allowing our subjects to erase crippling engrams associated with self-destructive behaviors and, when necessary, to rewrite their memories. Example: Joey D., a thirty-three-year-old heroin addict of fifteen years, has erased much of his craving for the drug within the past three months; though aware that he was once drug-dependent, he now gives every evidence of possessing less than thirty percent of the psycho-physiological traces for the substance formerly found in his pleasure receptors.

Secondly, through *psychopedagogy*: through instructions in the philosophy of New Realism developed by the founding director of the Mimecom Corporation, Anton Kreutzer. Though inspired by the philosophical and religious traditions of both West and East, New Realism is neither a bargain-basement philosophy, nor a synthetic religion. It is, rather, a carefully crafted assemblage of productive attitudes toward physical and social reality whose truth content is experimentally verifiable, and whose application can be learned by anyone above the age of seven. Example: Mary C., a twenty-eight-year-old compulsive pickpocket, transformed her world view within a week. She is now a junior stockbroker at a major Los Angeles investment house.

THE PALM AT THE END OF THE MIND / BEYOND THE LAST THOUGHT, RISES / IN THE BRONZE DECOR. *KOREDE IKIMASHO! BANZAI!*

the

Thirdly (and this is currently the most experimental of our procedures), through *psychocybernetics*. Through individual and group interface with instructional programs and data banks, our subjects may develop mental skills hitherto outside the range of their unenhanced capacities, and may even, in some cases, retain those skills outside the learning environment. Example: Dan P., a sixteen-year-old retarded adolescent with an intelligence quotient of 45 and a conduct disorder, was able to learn simple arithmetical computations within two and a half months. He is now a stock clerk.

Relevant technical literature is attached. The research of the Mimecom Corporation has been duplicated by outside experimenters and funded by the Department of Defense.

Of more immediate importance to you, however, is the application of the procedures outlined above to the curing of our social ills.

They are increasing, of course, at a prodigious and terrifying rate. The domestic turmoil of the last decade — divisions over the Vietnam War, assassinations of political leaders, urban riots, failure of the Great Society — have brought vast sectors of our population to the point of exhaustion or explosion. Pathologies of crime, poverty, addiction, and suicide waste the body politic, while the disintegration of the family and overloading of the educational system keep pace. I need hardly underline for you, a public official, the financial costs imposed on our society by these maladies. They are staggering. But in spite of the hundreds of billions of dollars spent on treatment, our disorders remain, seemingly, intractable. Not one program of relief devised by Right or Left, Republican or Democratic Party, private or public sector, can point to impressive success. At best, we see the most localized, most limited of results achieved by the ever-growing battalions of mental-health professionals and others of my colleagues among the "care providers." Whatever success stories they have to tell may be likened to spooning water from the sea.

Enough. It is time to set out on a new course, the only course that may stem the tide, a course that has the demonstrated potential to be both cost-conscious and humanly profitable. Instead of training armies of social workers to wade up to their necks in an ocean of human misery, we are well along the way toward turning our clients into fully empowered individuals whose collective existence will constitute an archipelago of hope. In the long run, the Mimecom Corporation can probably recover the costs of its investment in public service, through sales of technology rights, donations from grateful ex-clients, licensing agreements on franchise clinics, etc. But for the present, seed money is required. Large-scale benefits to the public cannot follow from our clinical prototype until its operations are expanded and refined. As noted above, our research laboratories have received federal support. But given the present U.S. Administration's domestic agenda, with its emphasis on the transfer of federal funds to the states, and their own health-and-welfare programs, we think it appropriate to apply for clinical funding on the state level.

We are not asking for a substantial amount. One million dollars per clinic, for a year-long trial run in five California cities, should be sufficient. That five million dollars is less than one percent of the total spent in a year on such failed institutions as prisons, social-welfare agencies, and mental hospitals.

What we are offering is in full accord with the best American traditions: a private initiative with a minimum of public outlay and a maximum of public benefit. Our partnership of limited government funding and private management can be a triumph for the administration of our state and provide a model of social service to the nation. It can, finally, make available the most efficient, and effective, means to help our country fulfill those goals annunciated in the preamble to the Constitution: "to form a more perfect union, establish justice, and insure domestic tranquility."

Thank you.

Tobias Schenkl, M.D.

US Consulate
Office of the Consulate General
Kyoto, Japan

February 26, 1974

Dear Tony,

Today I took the bus to the university, and what do you think I saw? Another housewife reading a tattered copy of *Synthiotics* — the Japanese edition, of course. She had a small boy with her, about five years old, her son I suppose. It made me realize for the first time how there must be a whole legion of children, the boy's age and younger, who are growing up as Syntheists. You have made your mark, Tony. The question I have now is, what next? Author, preacher — I can see you as the utopian ruler of a small country in the tropics, maybe wearing an olive drab Nehru jacket with lots of medals, a kind of capitalist Castro. Aha, that's it! You're the newly elected King of California! Setting out to colonize the stars. . .

But that's not the reason I'm writing. I have to tell somebody — you, of course. I'm in love. It's my teacher at the University, Eli Levitt. He is a bit mysterious — claims to be an American, but his accent is distinctly British. I don't know which is real yet. Most of the foreigners teaching in Kyoto are here because they couldn't get tenure at home, but Eli Levitt is different, more of a renegade crusader. He reminds me a little of you, in fact. Lately I've been hearing rumors that he left Ann Arbor in disgrace after demonstrating at some quasi-libertarian political fiasco where several underage co-eds were arrested in the nude. He is handsome, wreckless, aggressive, a sensualist with a razor-sharp, dangerous mind. Walt Whitman on steroids. I sing the body electric!

The day I met him we went for a walk after class and ended up fucking on the table at a local noodle shop while the owner slept behind the counter. It was my first time — well, you know what I mean. But it really was — my first time. And it's been like that ever since. We meet, eat, fuck, eat, sleep, fuck. I type for him sometimes. When I do there is something sexual about the way my fingers jab the keys. I can't study, or read, or even think. My brain has become a sex organ. I am all body. I love the smell of myself. I love the way I feel. I touch myself, pretending it is him, and my skin leaps with the thrill of lust.

The body. What a discovery. Why is it you never told me of these things? I thought we told each other everything.

He has read your book. When he saw it on the shelf in my room he threw it into the trash, saying that Synthiotics was a social disease and you were the Typhoid Mary of the seventies. He said that Nazism was immoral, but that Synthiotics is worse because it is amoral, nothing less than a return to primordial chaos. Beyond good and evil indeed! When I told him I was your sister he was irate, but I think it turned him on too. Since the incident he has been rougher with me, but also more jealous and possessive — neither of which I mind in the least! I want nothing more than to be a part of this man, to be subsumed by him, consumed by him.

I would do anything.

Yesterday I told him I was pregnant, just to see what he would do. He punched a hole in the wall, then he asked me to marry him. I started my period that night, while we were fucking. He cried! How my head spun! I felt so powerful. I am madly, crazily in love.

Love,
Josie

Wild Palms Group

SPONSORS:

Edmund G. Brown, Jr.

Michael Eisner

William Gates

Sen. John Glenn

Phillip Johnson

Henry Kissinger

Daniel K. Ludwig

Robert MacNamara

H. Ross Perot

Ted Turner

September 22, 1978

Dear Friend:

If you're like me — indeed, if you're like any of the accomplished individuals whose names appear on this page — you are feeling a profound sense of unease with what's happening in our country these days.

The nation is in free-fall, and from the comments and prescriptions being offered by our nation's leaders, there is no telling whether any of them has a clue about when, or how, or even if we are going to right ourselves. Our inner cities are free-fire zones. Vigilantism is on the rise. Lawbreaking has become a way of life, even among the wealthiest and most privileged members of society. Our children are neglected both intellectually and spiritually. Though we still have the highest GNP in the world, our infrastructure is crumbling, and our international competitiveness is rapidly eroding. And our leaders respond with cynicism and deceit, with lies and placebos. And yet . . .

And yet this need not be the case. When you listen, as I have, to people around the country — probably when you listen to yourself, and your family, and your friends — you realize and understand that people want something better. You know that people want calm and order and stability, want to live in harmony with one another, want more than anything the simple pleasures of home and hearth that peace and prosperity provide. And now, with seemingly daily breakthroughs in science and technology, we stand on the verge of being able to deliver those very blessings for one and all. If . . .

If we don't allow the chaos to swallow us. If we — the forward-thinking people of this land — don't stick our heads in the sand and allow the most spiritually bankrupt elements of our society to suck the rest of us into a dog-eat-dog world where we are doomed to a cycle of endless envy, selfishness, and war.

Plainly these are desperate times. Neither party has the answer. Politics as usual will not suffice when people stand at the point of no return. It is crucial that people who believe as we do act, and act now. It is crucial that we take responsibility.

I have written this letter to you because you have proven your leadership abilities in the most dynamic sectors of society. From Silicon Valley to Madison Avenue, from Hollywood to the Pentagon, from Wall Street to Capitol Hill, you have proven yourselves as visionaries in your chosen fields. This is not flattery on my part; our circumstances have placed us well beyond the point of flattery. Acknowledging our vital responsibilities, we have formed a group we call the Fathers (don't worry, women are welcome). We will be meeting at Wild Palms next February to discuss what should be done — drastic measures, if necessary. We must begin to dismantle the archaic structures and methods in place today and replace them with a new reality. We very much hope you will join us.

Sincerely yours,

Tony Kreutzer
Rancho Mirage, California

THE MIDNIGHT OATH OF THE FATHERS

[Nowhere was the response to Kreutzer and the tenets of New Realism more emphatic than in the divisive former republics of Yugoslavia. Reprinted here is the translation of an internal document from NSK, a group who until the rise of Synthiotics worldwide, had remained in relative obscurity in their native Slovenia.]

FATHERS!

IT IS MIDNIGHT. YOUR TIME, YOU WHO BLESS WITH BLOOD. ALL ANXIETY DESERTS US. THE PULSE OF PAIN IS A WALTZ, AND THROUGH FIRE WE WALK TALL. YOU, THE TRANSMITTER WHO COMES WITH POWER, ARE WHY WE DON'T GIVE IN TO THE HEART WHEN WE INFLICT SUFFERING. VIRGINS RAPED BY US WILL SING AND ACCOMPANY US TO THE GRAVE. WHERE ARE YOU, COMMANDMENTS? WHERE ARE YOU, PUNISHMENT? IT IS MIDNIGHT. YOUR TIME. YOU WHO BLESS WITH BLOOD. HOW BEAUTIFUL IS YOUR FACE!

TODAY WE TRANSFORM ALL THE VERMIN OF THE MARSHLANDS. ALL THE BEASTS OF THE FOREST, ALL THE DISEASES OF THE HEART, INTO INCENSE. WE INHALE THE SMELLS OF SUFFERING AND DESPAIR, AND WE FOLLOW YOU, POSSESSOR OF OUR AFTERLIFE. WE RETURN HOME WITH SNAKES, AND WHEN WE APPEAR, OUR CHILDREN CURSE THE DAY THEY WERE CONCEIVED, AND OUR WOMEN REND THEIR CLOTHES, CUTTING INTO THEIR WHITE FLESH TO AVERT US FROM OUR INTENTIONS. O KREATOR, GIVE US POWER THAT THE MISFORTUNE OF OUR LIVES BE WORTHY OF YOUR GREATNESS!

WE PRODUCE FLESH, AND GENERATE YOUR EDEN. YOU KNOW WHAT LOVE IS, AND SO YOU SOW EVIL, FOR EVIL IS IN THE FLESH, PSYCHE IS FLESH, AND FLESH IS ALL. AND FROM THIS EVIL, FROM THESE HYDROCARBONS OF ECSTASY, YOU OFFER US THE HOST WHICH RECOMBINES THE MOLECULES OF OUR BEING, AND WHEN THAT TRANSFORMATION HAPPENS, OUR BODIES WILL BECOME BLISS BEFORE YOU, ANNIHILATOR OF WORLDS.

IT IS MIDNIGHT. OUR TIME. WE WHO BLESS WITH BLOOD.

October 15, 1978

My dear Josie,

As you read this, I am gone. I didn't plan for this to happen, but when the offer came from Berkeley I could not make myself turn it down. Every day for the past month, I have thought about telling you, but I always found an excuse. When I picked up my airline ticket this morning, I began to realize that I was not going to tell you. Then, when I lingered in the market until three o'clock, when I knew you would be at the park with Grace, I realized I would leave without seeing you again.

By now you will have returned home. You will have noticed my lateness. Perhaps you will even have noticed the bare hangers in the closet and the two empty drawers. As I write I am sitting in the JAL departure lounge, waiting for a one-way flight to Tokyo, then home.

These years in Kyoto have been a kind of hibernation. I have heard of a species of frogs who bury themselves in a shroud of their own mucous membrane at the onset of a drought, then lie dormant until the rains return. That is me, though when I arrived, I did not expect my condition to ever change.

At first I thought you were the perfect companion to me — we were both animals. Love, lust, made us angry and stupid. The best part of sex was how depraved it made us feel, whether we were teacher and student, father and daughter, Great White Hunter and poor native girl, the decrepit sensualist and the arctic hysteric. Yet, for all that urgent humping and scratching, when the lights came on I was a dirty old man and you were frigid. I made it my job to "melt" you. This was no act of kindness.

When we were married, I thought I would stay in Kyoto for the rest of my life. I looked forward to watching the decline of civilization from my comfortable academic armchair. You seemed like the ideal end-of-the-world companion, the perfect someone with whom to share this slow, pedestrian apocalypse. Your awakening sexuality could have been the side-effect of radiation poisoning, a vaginal death rattle. It somehow never occurred to me that you — that we — were fertile.

When Grace was born my feelings for you changed. Things I used to find perversely exciting began to revolt me. The way you used to laugh in your sleep. Your explosive rages. The obscene phone calls to my secretary (I always knew it was you). The daily letters to your brother. The way I'd wake up to find you gnawing my fingernails. Some of these things about you began to make me queasy.

About that time my friends back home in Berkeley and Michigan began to drop hints that Tony Kreutzer was beginning to do some of his own lobbying in Washington on behalf of Mimecom, making friends, doing favors around town, scoping out things on Capitol Hill. They urged me to return, to help lay the groundwork for an anti-Kreutzer campaign should he make a move. But I reasoned that I would be more effective here — with you. I must confess, I spent many an afternoon turning our apartment upside down looking for his letters to you. I never found them.

The letters. I have always imagined that you and Tony were lovers, as impossible as that may sound. At first I welcomed the odd humiliation of it, the irony of my strange position. I even wrote to my friends back in the States that I had learned Kreutzer molested his sister. I never mentioned that I was married to her! In a way, our marriage was a kind of insurance against any rash, sentimental impulse I might have to return home. But that was before Grace.

In the end, it is the love I feel for our little girl that has awakened me. I feel myself alive again, and if I am alive I must go down fighting. There is no place for you and Grace in my "real" life. My life as a man of action. You wouldn't know me, Josie. You have never met the man I used to be, the one I will be again by the time you read this letter. It hurts me to leave my daughter, but I don't have the heart, nor perhaps the right, to separate a mother and daughter forever, and it is my deepest wish never to see you again.

I am sorry for that, Josie. I truly am. But it is best. I am sorry for the unfairness of it all. I am sorry for your pain. I once told you your brother was amoral. Well, I am immoral. I do wrong, Josie. I do it knowingly. I will even do everything within my power to avoid the consequences of my actions.

The world is in trouble. We have come to a time when it is impossible to do good. Right now the task at hand is to rediscover what is right and true, and to fight for it. The next generation, perhaps, can lead lives that will be better than ours.

Goodbye,
Eli

Josie
We are epic — two generals who happen to be on opposing sides. It was always that way with us, even in bed. A holy war; that's why it was so good. I did what I had to.
Eli
What do we do now, Josie? Settle down in the suburbs and barbecue by the pool? Fly to Vegas and get hitched like Elvis and Priscilla? Why the reunion, Josie?
Josie
I'll tell you why. Because. . . I am parched. My brother loves the desert, not I: I want the flood. To touch you, to taste you. . . smell you. To start the holy war all over again —

He stands, goes to her, lifts her from chair — she's helpless. He kisses her deeply.

I lay on the mat on the floor of my cell hating my body. It was nothing personal. Objectively speaking, my body was no more contemptible than another. It was just that I couldn't get out. It lay there like a donkey, helplessly expanding and contracting, locked into the brute cycle of breath and blood, bound in its sinews, squeezed tight by its own tensed muscle, smothered by fat, pulled taut in the hideously sensate and tensile grip of its nervous system.

I wished I could sprout a hundred eyes, all of them rising from my body on long sensing feelers. I wished a thousand mouths could issue from my throat, a thousand tiny jaws on insect legs to travel through the night-dark monastery into every cell, to impregnate every sleeping monk, through orifice or pore, to eat him from the inside out and then come back to me.

My divorce from Eli was complete. I had come to the monastery to regenerate, but so far I had failed. I tried to think of my child — our child — but I could only conjure her image standing in a field of graves, swathed in the cold gauze of thought. She was looking down, twining her hair around a finger and holding something in her hand. At the sight of her, there was a painful impulse in my abdomen, naked and undefended as a low moan. And as unseemly. My pelvis sprouted teeth and bit it off. Poor Grace, poor little girl. An aborted moan, unable to die yet unable to leave the graveyard. A serious child. The only photograph I had of her at that point was taken at her first birthday party; surrounded by grinning adults and plates of cake, she bowed her head before the camera, her sideways expression one of stunned preternatural intelligence, her tiny forehead knit in a struggle with dimly apprehended dread. I called to her from across the graveyard but she did not look up. Another throb rose in my lower body, plaintive and reed-like, as though emerging through a stran-gle-hold. It quivered faintly and

expired. I stepped sideways and fell away from her, back into my body. Eli was there, his smell, his spoor, dripping off organ and bone. Again, the terrible liquid moan of feeling rose in my pelvis, lapping at me like a frightened dog. I struck at it and fled, mashing my face against the fibrous fatty outer limit of my body, clawing it to no avail. I imagined a spider executing its short fatal pounce, its elemental circuitry a miracle of concentration and release, its movement express-ing, in a nanosecond, the tri-umphant gloat of total carnal possession performed with the mechanical efficiency of a nerve function. Its act of penetration and devouring stripped of the usual gross creaturous excess that accompanies such acts — no hot breath, no fierce rub of the tongue, no rending teeth to affirm in one last moment of shocking con-tact the idiotic agreement: you and I are the same, you have a heart, I have a heart, you eat me, I become you. There is no heart. Just the pounce, just the blood, just the dull and savage elec-tricity.

I opened my eyes. I was still on the mat, on the floor. I closed them and tunneled through the dark. It was a familiar dark.

It had been with me all my life, although I had not always been cog-nizant of it. In college I had been aware of it but only as a strongly sensed place that I left when I woke in the morning. Before I opened my eyes I felt it lingering about me, a seductive heaviness that went beyond the weight of sleep pulling on my limbs as I poised to enter the day. At that

moment the rolling dark at my back was more real in its fading presence than the spectral abstracts that were my daily activities. I would try to prolong the moment, to turn and see where it was that I had come from, but I could only see the awful furniture of my alleged life — my classes, my projects, my friends — objects void of meaning in rela-tion to my secret place.

Now, in the monastery I had fall-en into it and burrowed. Eli wasn't there. As deeply as he had pene-trated, he had not gotten this far, my deepest home.

Eli wasn't there. My hated body wasn't there. But I was not alone. I sensed various beings present in the dark, moving around me. I heard the occasional low grunt, the snap of a small bone. I smelled them or perhaps smelled their prey, years of rank, rotting offal. Although in the outer world I can-not bear a stink, this smell consoled and soothed me. It was big and warm enough to sit in, to wrap around me like a blanket of safety. No one could ever get me here.

In this I luxuriated, rolling and snuggling and kicking, curling and uncurling my toes. I sank deeper, as if into thick, velvety blood, all suf-fused with a vibratory sonorous pumping. It was like the inside of a huge heart. The massive tissues of it opened and closed around me, the opening a rapid expansion of night sky, the closing a secret mud cave, a tied-up dirty sack. And at the root of it the powerful tug of the deep earth crawling with end-less vitality, the joie de vivre of the headless insect population, the ground bones, the eternal hair and claws of all the dead.

But whose heart?

There were teeth and eyes; I felt rather than heard the answer. Rather than a body, its form was aggression delineated, destruction for its own sake, something like fire but with brains and will. It snatched my breath, but only for a moment. What do you want? I asked.

To eat your bones.

I could give you something bette
than bones, I offered. You woul
soon be done with my bones
There's much more to be had on th
outside. You could have it throug
me.

I've been eating you all your life
I'll keep eating you until you'r
dead. Then I'll move on.

I imagined its teeth in m
intestines, my blood and shit pour
ing into my bowels, poisoning me.
sensed it, huge and stony but wit
striking power, its eyes brimming
with malevolence dislocated from
emotion, its jagged teeth each a
totem of devouring. I tried a differ
ent approach. Are you angry at me
Do you hate me?

No.

Have I harmed you? Have
deprived you of life by keeping you
down here?

No answer.

If you joined with me there woul
be more pleasure for you. I coul
feed you and feed you.

I don't want pleasure. I only wan
death.

You must be angry if you only
want death. For an instant I fel
maternal sympathy in my breasts
Why are you angry?

I'm not angry. I'm not human.

Its eyes went hot and inanimate
as radiation, its huge bulk fixed a
rock.

I felt cheated. Alright, I said. Bu
let me see what's behind you. I
there is something behind you, le
it come out.

Immediately there was wavering
color and blurred movement as a
cacophany of forms, all aswarm
each other, fought to achieve meta-
morphosis. Horns, hooves, faces
tails and paws took shape and dissolved before they fully incarnated
A griffin, a dragon, a cobra, a lizard
the dull stupid visage of a rhino —
for a moment I even thought I saw
the sweet limpid face of a unicor
glimmering through the protea
mess. Then the flux of shape
became a slow muddy pull out o
which. . . stepped a rather beautifu
young man wet with membrane
The monster's son blinked his dar
eyes bashfully. He looked at me.
looked at him. I thought: Of course
The male. I smiled and extended my
hand. "Come here," I said.

the face of POWER

by Peter Katz

reprinted from <u>New West</u> magazine, August 6, 1980

The excitement surrounding the Senatorial candidacy of Tony Kreutzer has neared hysteria in the past six weeks. To hear much of the media tell it, Kreutzer is our silver-haired Moses, come to lead us to a promised land that only he has glimpsed. He has been feted at the Esalen Institute and hailed as a saviour in some of the most conservative enclaves in Orange County. As of this writing, he is fourteen points ahead in the polls, and his campaign has had remarkable success in painting the opposition as a reactionary and religiously intolerant "timid minority."

But there is more to Kreutzer's candidacy than meets the eye. His history reveals a callous, grasping man, for whom the only fundamental truth is his own ambition.

The origins of Kreutzer's power, with Mimecom and Dex Wyckoff, the brilliant and ill-fated neurobiologist, are well known. Perhaps less apocryphal is the consensus of all who knew Wyckoff: that suicide was simply not in his character. "The only reason I can see him doing it," said one friend, "would be to see what was on the other side. Or because he already knew."

The official account is that Wyckoff shot himself, and subsequent investigations have found no cause to dispute this. But Wyckoff's longtime assistant, Michael Naimark, claims to have seen Kreutzer leaving Wyckoff's lab shortly after hearing the blast. And though he says he told his story repeatedly to investigators, the police now have no record of it.

What is indisputable is the explosive acceleration ever since in Kreutzer's enterprises. Virtually all of Mimecom's patents are in Wyckoff's name, and its gleaming offices are now as ubiquitous as Synthiotic street clinics in America's cities. And though nominally independent, their operations are in fact so closely intertwined that Kreutzer has had to fend off continual allegations that Synthiotics' tax-exempt status shields Mimecom profits. "Our position," said IRS agent Sanford Stone, "is that they are two sides of the same coin." But the courts have yet to agree, and Kreutzer, whose personal worth is estimated in the tens of millions, has sidestepped the issue this campaign season by putting his holdings in a blind trust.

More disturbing is Kreutzer's penetration into the upper reaches of government. The growing number of lawsuits, stemming from the vigilante tactics regularly dispensed by New Realists in dealing with the homeless, has done little damage to their popularity with the general public. Nor has it affected Synthiotics' accountability for its growing share of the public health budget. Indeed, Kreutzer has become one of the city's unofficial and elite decision-makers, a fixture at Jerry Brown's parties and, thanks to his Japanese connections, a major player in the resurgence of downtown Los Angeles.

While serving up a feel-good message for public consumption on the eve of his campaign, Kreutzer has in fact strengthened his grip on the government through the Fathers. Though not exactly an underground organization, they conduct their affairs with Masonic secrecy, state-of-the-art communications and information-gathering systems, and a security apparatus that some say amounts to a private army.

There have also been sketchy but unignorable reports of a link between the Fathers and the spate of childnappings that have terrorized affluent areas around LA recently. In one incident, Robert Birnbaum, a former Kreutzer employee, was arrested for the kidnapping of a three-year-old girl in San Marino. At first, concerned that he not be thought of as a sex offender, he indicated that he was acting on orders from higher-ups, and telephone records from jail show that he called several Synthiotics numbers. Freed on bail the next day, Birnbaum has since disappeared

Kreutzer, however, has denied any involvement. "Birnbaum was a damaged person, a paranoiac, and a regrettable failure for the movement," he said in a prepared statement. "But we repudiate any implication of Synthiotic involvement with either the kidnapping or his disappearance. There are many enemies on the way to the garden."

(cont'd on page 181)

Paige
The Senator entered politics in the late Seventies. Back then, my father was a well-respected journalist. To him, the Senator was a dangerous man, a demagogue. He wrote a series of articles tying Kreutzer and Synthiotics to a shadowy vigilante group — it cost the Senator the election. Men broke into the house and took me away. I was three years old —

Harry
The Fathers. . .

Paige
I never saw my parents again; I was raised in New Realist foster homes.

UNTIL YESTERDAY I'D GONE 35 YEARS WITHOUT SEEING SOMEONE BEAT UP. IT ACTUALLY LOOKED LIKE ONE OF THOSE STUPID ROBERT LONGO PAINTINGS

[The following transcript dates from Kreutzer's first and unsuccessful Senatorial candidacy. It was originally broadcast as a statewide infomercial on October 12, 1980.]

They say I am mad, but I am not mad, and soon they'll be changing their tune. All those dead souls with their noses to the grindstone of the sacred bottom line always call the visionaries madmen until shares in the dream start trading on the Big Board, and for Mimecom, that day's not far off.

They say I am a Don Quixote tilting at the windmill of the two-party system. You can't beat the old Democrat-Republican shell-game that's kept the suckers hypnotized looking for the little pea while their pockets are being picked for a hundred years. That's reality, Tony, is what they say. That's *realpolitik*. You're wasting your time, you're wasting your money, you're wasting your spiritual energy. Be realistic, you are going to lose!

Well, maybe I'm going to lose the election this time around, and maybe I'm not. But what they call *realpolitik*, what they call reality, is just some dumb sitcom that's about to be cancelled. Realists is what they think they are, and that's what the dinosaurs thought too, I suppose, about the time that asteroid got dropped on their heads. What's all this mammal stuff, it'll never get off the ground. You can't beat the old saurian reality, it's been around for a hundred million years.

They just don't get it. They don't get the New Realism. They think I've got to change reality to win this election, and they don't see how that's possible. But I've already done it — win, lose, or draw!

The Democrats and the Republicans just can't see that. In their reality, winning the election is the only reality, the end which justifies all the usual sleazeball means, so they can't comprehend the New Reality, in which this Senatorial election is only one means to accomplish . . . much higher ends.

Through Synthiotic street clinics and foster homes, through mass spiritual enlightenment, I have freed a generation of lost souls of every race, creed, and national origin from the drugs and poverty, and from the despair and degradation of our own post-industrial inner cities. That's a whole lot more important than whether I win the election or not this time around, and if this campaign moves that great work forward, I've won the victory already.

Now a lot of good people, people who do understand the New Realism, they say, Tony, why are you throwing your time and your money and your enormous spiritual energy down the unseemly dirty rathole of this Senatorial campaign?

All the good you've done, and these Democratic-Republicans and their mercenary sleazeball media samurai are calling you a kiddie-snatcher, a cultist, a vigilante unilateralist, a Jap-lover, and a whole lot worse.

You're a successful science fiction writer. You've founded Synthiotics. You're building a great corporate enterprise in Mimecom. You don't have to do this for a living. Why are you willing to get down there and mudwrestle for votes with your pygmy-intellect opponents?

Sure, I could run Mimecom and Synthiotics and write a few more books and sniff the flowers and rest on my laurels and clip my coupons and consider my great life's work already done.

But that's twentieth century thinking, my friends, and I am a man of the Twenty-first. The Twentieth century mind slumbers on in the belief that there is a single reality, a linear progression of events from the past through the present and on into the future like shish-kebab on a skewer. But the Twenty-first century mind is awake to the infinite realities of the great multiverse of space and time.

I live in that virtual reality, folks, the reality of the Twenty-first century. And from that perspective, it's this reality which doesn't seem real. It drives me crazy to see the American people staggering around like zombies in a dumb dream-world sitcom produced for them by the military-media-political-industrial-medical complex, when the universe awaits them.

That's why I created Synthiotics — to wake up individuals one by one. And that's why I founded Mimecom, whose great mission it is to free the American people from the single-reality media monopoly Disney-world of the mind that you've been tricked into buying as your own collective American Dream. And to bring about the media millennium, where every American is free to inhabit a reality of his or her own choosing, through the software science of the mind and the hardware technology of the spirit!

And that's why I'm running for the United States Senate, my friends! Because there are all sorts of mean-spirited and powerful people out there who don't want that to happen! Who will do anything to stop me from freeing this great nation from its long nightmare sleep. Media mavens! Washington politicians! Captains of industry! Even people who call themselves freedom fighters!

There's a vast conspiracy out there to crush Tony Kreutzer, and Synthiotics, and Mimecom, and keep you from awakening from their slave-master's dream.

That's their conspiracy, my friends. The conspiracy of the single-reality past against the multiple-reality future. The conspiracy of the dying old against the birth of the new.

But we are the New Realists, and we have our conspiracy too.

For as the poet said, "Could thou and I but with fate conspire, to seize this sorry scheme of things entire, would we not shape it closer to the heart's desire?"

Why not?

With Synthiotics and Mimecom, we have proven that we can.

And with your votes, I will.

notes from the underground

Friends! A cruel struggle is now beginning. The time has come when we are compelled to fight against a determined and merciless enemy. But we live at a crucial turning-point in human history. We are the shock-troops of reality at a time when everywhere reality is threatened. We are the friends of hope and freedom now that society has entered its final, fateful phase.

As the market has expanded into every crevice on the globe and reached into every crinkle in the brain, it has turned what was solid into shadow, and what was real into spectacle. From the mass production of objects, the market has moved on to the mass manufacture of images and dreams, laboratory products delivered directly into our own nervous systems. The market may seem natural and transparent, the product of an invisible hand, but behind it there is an opaque and unnatural entity at its core. Hidden but active, this entity seeks to manipulate the consumer — formerly the citizen — and to exert power through the state apparatus of coercion, the ideological apparatus of religion, and the media apparatus of the spectacle itself. That opaque and unnatural entity is Realitician Anton Kreutzer.

When the Founding Fathers wrote the Constitution and the Bill of Rights, they had no conception of the extent to which power would be concentrated in our times or of the extent to which it would be globalized. They had no inkling of the terrible power which would be exerted by today's bureaucratic warfare state, by the organized institution of the syncretistic church, or by the multinational media and infotainment corporation — let alone by all three working together in close but secret co-ordination.

This growth of centralized power has far outstripped the democratic institutions that our predecessors founded. Rather we have come to feel that these democratic institutions themselves are now no more than instruments in the hands of powerful, hidden entities.

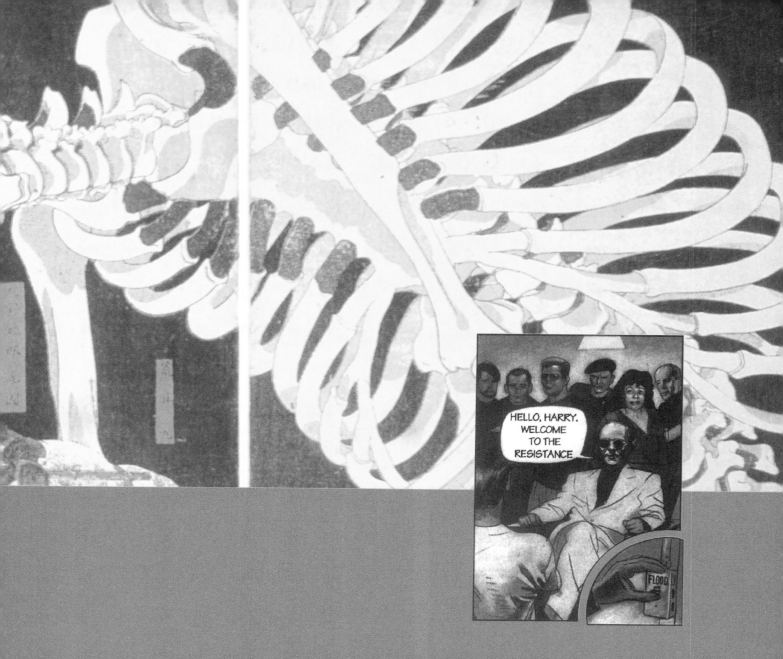

Paradoxically, it is precisely this sense of public powerlessness that Anton Kreutzer is able to manipulate for his own private ends by offering the vision of a new kind of society, in which it would no longer be necessary for us to choose or think or feel for ourselves, except within the parameters he himself has set. Thus out of powerlessness, he builds his power; out of our confusion, he builds his purpose; out of our reality, he builds his dream — and persuades us it is ours.

What must we do to combat this monstrous concentration of power in state, cult, and spectacle? How can we become active citizens and dreamers rather than passive recipients of the dreams he has manufactured for us?

The whole edifice of global postmodernity within which he thrives must be undermined and overthrown. We must look for the pressure points in the armature of his new empire. We must find the contradictions in the deployment of his new logic. We must exploit the flaws in the psychology of his New Realism. We must be everywhere and nowhere. We must gather in the hidden places of his empire and conceal ourselves in the innermost centers of his power. Our aim must be to undo everything he has done and to rebuild from ground zero a world in which what is real is what is desirable.

Friends! There is not much time left. We must act swiftly. But we must also find the time to look around us at objects of beauty, to contemplate, and to read about the past. Our struggle will be in vain if we do not succeed in saving a sense of the beauty of reality and the meaning of history. It is our precious responsibility to preserve the channel of truth running unbroken between past Enlightenment and future Emancipation, between our mentors and our children. May the Friends prevail! We are the shock-troops of reality! Destroy Anton Kreutzer! Keep hope alive!

THE MORE MONKEYS THE BETTER

MEMORANDUM

Date: 3 April, 1981
To: File
From: TK
Re: Ito Industries limited partnership
Raw transcript — scheduled telephone conference

Telephone conference between myself and Masahiro Ito. Simultaneous translation to be provided by Ito Industries. Josie Kreutzer Levitt will be present as a silent observer, monitoring the translation via listening extension. Japanese portion of this tape to be translated and transcribed for the records by Mimecom support services in Los Angeles.

Kreutzer: Hello? Hello? Mr. Ito! Anton Kreutzer. I'm very pleased to be speaking with you at — Where's the translator? There's no translator on this line. Just a moment, Mr. Ito. Josie, take the phone. Tell me what this guy is saying.

Josie: He says he's sorry about the translator. You're such a great businessman he assumed you spoke Japanese. I wasn't supposed to repeat that part. He doesn't know I'm your sister. He thinks I'm Japanese.

Kreutzer: Good! This is good!

Josie: Should I tell him?

Kreutzer: Not yet. Yes — tell him. Tell him you're my sister and you are Japanese. It might play into our hand if he's a little mystified.

Josie: [laughs] He's asking what you wanted to discuss.

Kreutzer: What were you laughing at? What did he say?

Josie: He made me promise not to repeat it.

Kreutzer: Great — never mind. I want to propose a meeting to discuss a joint venture between Mimecom and Ito Industries. I'm holding patents on some flight simulator technology that was recently declassified by the U.S. military, and I'm interested in discussing applications for the home entertainment industry.

Josie: He's asking if you mean virtual reality.

Kreutzer: No, no, much more sophisticated than that. This stuff is user-transparent. No headsets, no goggles, none of that techy stuff . . . Josie? Josie?

Josie: I'm sorry. We were talking about *The Manchurian Candidate*. It's his favorite film. Have you seen it?

Kreutzer: What? No.

Josie: Neither have I, but I'm faking it pretty well. Have your secretary get a copy and watch it.

Kreutzer: What do you think? Will he take a meeting? Tell him we'll give him a live demonstration that'll blow his mind.

Josie: He says he's not interested in a partnership but he'll look at your presentation. His mother reads your books. He says you are a visionary.

Kreutzer: Ha! What a crock of shit! Good, good. Tell him I say he couldn't be more wrong. Americans are bunglers, that's our stock in trade. We've mastered the art of making mistakes. It's called creativity.

Josie: He says you're too modest.

Kreutzer: Way too modest. Tell him my R&D philosophy has always been to increase the margin of error wherever possible. The more monkeys you have typing, the better. Tell him that.

Josie: He says he understands.

Kreutzer: What was the rest of that?

Josie: I had to explain about the typing monkeys.

Kreutzer: Jesus H. Christ! Okay, now tell him I've got the monkeys if he's got the typewriters.

Josie: Tony, I don't think this is the right way —

Kreutzer: Just tell him!

Josie: Alright!

(pause)

Kreutzer: Hey . . . hey! Josie! What are you saying to the old bird? I thought he understood about the monkeys.

Josie: Just hold on.

Kreutzer: Hold on? I'm the one having this conversation, Josie. Josie? You're fired. Wait, don't hang up!

Josie: He's invited us to his house for the weekend.

Kreutzer: Us?

[NOTE from trans. dept.: Orig. tape erased. No verification of trans. avail.]

DADDY?

What I did on my summer
vacation By Grace Ito

This summer we went on a 6
day cruise for my birthday.
It was a Lot of fun because I
was the only kid and I didn't have
to play any sports. I read the
Diary of Anne Frank And all of
the Wizard of OZ books.
We stopped in Athens to pick up
Uncle Tony. He didn't bring me
a present. When I asked him why
he pointed to the stars and said,
they're your present and when
you're bigger I'll take you there.
I didn't Like him. He was sweaty
and he had make-up on to make
him look tan.
Papa Ito was mad, I played rummy
with the cook, and he said "we're

in Tel Aviv" (not Athens). Mother
said it was because the crew
Lives in a different world and
I shouldn't visit them in case
I wouldn't be able to come back,
Like Dorothy in the Wizard of Oz
Papa Ito gave me a book by
Lao Tsu and mother gave me
an ivory necklace.
I wrote a poem but I threw
it in the ocean

Grace
You know what Japan is,
Harry? A pretty little girl
who throws up to stay thin.
Post-suicidal musings, by
Grace Wyckoff. . . When I
was little, Mama used to
take me to Hiroshima for
kabuki. There was one
about this deformed
princess — born with her
hand in a fist. Someone
turned her into a whore. . .

Harry
Why did you do it, Grace?

Grace
Why? Because we like you.
(beat)
I feel like an animal that
knows it's going to die. . .
(as she traces her bandage
with a finger)
Full of ghosts, kabuki.
Always loved the ghosts;
never scared me.
(beat)
They scare me now,
Harry. They scare me now.

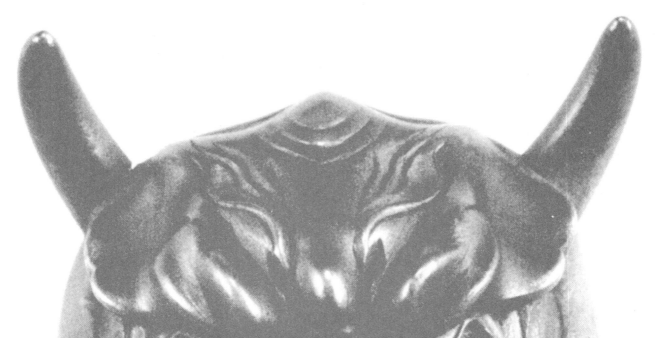

[The following is an excerpt from a letter Grace Wyckoff wrote to her father, Eli Levitt. It was never mailed.]

I have known of my weakness ever since May 14, 1984. Shall I tell you the story? I had just finished classes at the company school, and I wanted to catch a ride home in the family limo — I was half a foot taller than all of the Japanese girls in the third grade, and they shunned me as some huge, rugged monster with bitten fingernails and too much money. So I never took the school bus if I could get a ride with Papa Ito. I was less afraid of him than of those sylph-like girls with their long, dark braids and blank, moon-shaped faces. Ito treated me with an indifference that I found flattering at that awkward, conspicuous age.

The door to Papa Ito's office was open. Ito and mother knelt on the floor, facing each other. How long had they been there? All the petals had fallen from the branch of cherry blossoms on the low, lacquer table between them. Mother was motionless, her eyes fixed on the harbor afire with the sunset thirty floors below. Ito's eyes were fixed on nothing. I had never seen him with his mouth open so wide. The curved hilt of the sword jutted from his face like the horn of a marvelous unicorn.

I must have called for help, because people came. Mother never spoke, and she never moved. Her hands were bloody, and she held them folded in her lap, perfectly still. I knelt beside her and tried to be still — as still as she, as still as Papa Ito. I had a very strong sense, then as never before, of the three of us as a family. Sometime after dark they finished taking pictures and took the body away.

At home, mother called for a bottle of brandy and went to her room. I followed. She sat on her bed, measured half of the bottle into a tall glass, and downed it. Then she lay her head in my lap. For the next eight hours, she muttered, wept, laughed and slept by turns. The smell of blood was pungent in the room. I stroked her hair, and once, very briefly, she squeezed my hand. After eight hours, she went into the bathroom and ran some water. When she came back her hands were clean. Then she drank the other half of the bottle and fell into a deep sleep.

It was a long night for an eight-year-old girl. I felt important, and powerful, and helpless. My mother was an enchanted princess, trapped inside an evil-looking glass. Everything she touched turned to gold and died. Even Papa Ito.

I was so sad for us! As dawn broke, I had a desperate dream that you would come and take us away. I picked up the telephone and called information in twenty-seven different cities: none of the operators could find you for me.

The next day mother held a press conference. I watched her gaunt, hardened face on television as she announced that, as Ito's executor, she would be assuming control of all corporate holdings, etc. When one of the reporters asked her point blank if she had killed her husband, she just paused in silence for a moment, then went on with her prepared statement. I couldn't believe that this was the woman who had lain in my lap all the night through. Looking at her wrecked complexion, I knew her grief was beyond reproach — I also knew that she would not be crying again.

I spent the rest of the news conference throwing up in my *amah's* handbag.

It was then that I discovered my profound weakness as a human being. And do you know why, Father? Because I loved her. I loved her painfully. I never believed that she had killed him. I still don't. I don't think I'm capable of believing it. So you see? I'm not a good person, Father. I'm just too weak to hate.

Dearest Hiro:

It's a good thing you didn't come to the airport to see me off. Mother turned up at the last minute in a pink Chanel suit. Ugh! She looked dressed for an open casket. Mom, Lenin and Chairman Mao. Bon Voyage!

So here I am. Is it gauche to say I love Paris? Oh, but Paris loves _me_! It's light-hearted and bitter-sweet, worldly and forgiving. I feel at home, maybe for the first time in my life. Everywhere I go I feel like I'm wandering through the rooms of a house I've always lived in without knowing it.

Yesterday I ended up at the _Marché des Puces_—aha! This must be my closet! I bought a pair of pearl earrings for mother and a pair of brown alligator platforms from the thirties for me. I wore them last night with black leggings and a Gaultier vest. Too sexy! So I went out dancing→this morning I woke up to find a trail of blood leading from my bed all the way back to the elevator! I couldn't remember how I got home, and for a moment I thought I might be a murderess—until I found that the blood came from the blisters on my feet!

Do you miss me? I may never come back. Anastasia Romanoff and I are talking about sharing an apartment in the Latin Quarter.... Just kidding. I'd never abandon you.

Love Grace

3/4/89

Last night was another of those corporate dinner parties I'm always being forced to attend. The kind where the Japanese hosts serve something outrageous like Cheese Whiz on Ritz crackers with marshmallow salad, like that's what'll make Americans go orgasmic and buy three drillion of their electronic widgets or whatever it is they're trying to sell.

So there I am at the dreaded "children's table" that loathesome purgatory where anyone single and under twenty-five gets to suffer the humiliation of dining tête-a-tête with a bunch of three year-old management trainees and their nannies. Almost as humiliating as dining with the adults!

Anyway, this guy named Hiro is sitting across from me. (His father is one of mother's accountants or something.) The table is so low that I have to bend over to reach my plate, and every time I do Hiro looks down my bustier—which is where I just _happen_ to have my cigarettes stashed. When I went to the bathroom for a smoke I got out my lipstick and drew a heart with an arrow through it on the mirror. Then, when I got back to my seat, I passed Hiro the cigarettes under the table and _he_ went to the bathroom.... Well, he didn't say _anything_. He kept this poker face on for the rest of the evening. It wasn't until I got home that I found he'd slipped a piece of paper into the cellophane of my pack of cigarettes — on it a smiley face holding a gun to its temple!

FRONT   BACK

Point of entry   Exit wound

38

UNIVERSITY OF CALIFORNIA
APPLICATION FOR UNDERGRADUATE ADMISSION
AND SCHOLARSHIPS 1991–1992
Nonrefundable Fee Required: $40.00 for each campus.
Make check or money order payable to:

FOR UC USE ONLY

College to me means a chance to make what has been a good life into "the Good Life." By that I don't mean money, or fame, or even success as we know it. Success to me means looking back on it all and saying to my own son who is about to enter college, "Go for it, man!"

I have always done well in school. I'm one of those people teachers call "hard working." As I understand it that means "He's no genius, but at least he knows it." And that's okay by me. In addition to my B+ grade point average, you might consider my extracurricular accomplishments: In my sophomore year, I won a trip to Sacramento for an essay I submitted to the Warner Brothers "World Beyond War" essay contest. As a junior, I started an after-school Reggae/Dancehall Appreciation Club. In my senior year I was Chairman of the Yearbook Committee, as well as being voted "Most Likely to Find Bliss."

My ambitions in life are twofold: to be on the U.S. Olympic Wrestling Team, and to go to Law School.

There are two things you need to know about Harry Wyckoff to decide whether or not he is fit to join your institution: family and family. But Harry Wyckoff is an orphan, isn't he? What a strange thing for him to say. Let me explain.

Over the years I have had many loving families. I grew up in foster homes, most of which were kind and caring, and none of which really had an impact on me personally. But that doesn't mean I don't have a family. I have two families, both of whom taught me a great deal and made me whom I am today.

My first family is the Westminster YMCA Wrestling Team. I have been a member of that family since the sixth grade, when I lived with an air traffic controller at LAX and used to watch the planes take off to Japan through my bedroom window. Even when I lived in Pasadena, I took the bus every Friday evening for practice and spent the night with my teammate, Tommy Las-

zlo, who is like my brother (and who is also applying to UCLA).

Wrestlers are a special breed. Their code of ethics says "Be who you are, and don't let anyone you-know-what on your parade." It doesn't matter how you dress or where you're from: on the mat, no-one stands tall and everybody sweats.

Thus, while all my foster families were of a religious bent, I personally remained unaffected. I even learned tolerance from the experience of living with people of different points of view. And being part of the wrestling team has has taught me not to lay trips on anyone — including myself. I feel that this aspect of my background will make me a very receptive and open minded student at UCLA.

My second family has been the legal system. What a surprising twist...Let me explain that I grew up as a ward of the court. My "legal" father is a man in a black robe, and my mother wears a toga and a blindfold! They were good parents. Principled. Fair. Always with my best interests at heart.

Some people think our legal system exists mainly to give lawyers something to do. I think that if the legal system can give a kid with no parents a happy childhood, it's a pretty worthwhile institution, and one I'd be proud to be part of. I would like to be a lawyer in order to help other people like myself find their true families. At this point I plan to be an adoption advocate, although I also have a side interest in entertainment law.

So that's what going to college is all about for me. I don't think you could call me ambitious. It's not about money (well, not that much money), and I don't want to change the world. Life has treated me fine so far, and it probably always will. I just want to study hard, do well, earn my degree, and maybe along the way meet a nice girl — or two!

economics

Local Motion

Paige Katz, age 16, a resident at the SYNTHIOTICS YOUTH HOME, has reached Level Seven in the program (about a year ahead of time). And that's not all. She's also one of thirty students nationwide to receive a Synthiotics Special Achievement Award. New Realism Founder Tony Kreutzer will pin it on personally at a ceremony at the Home next Tuesday (February 14th — Valentine's Day) at 3:30. Way to go, Paige!

3 9

4/11/93

Dear Mr. Kreutzer,

Here, as per your request, is a photo that our operative took of Ms. Katz with Harry Wyckoff, a fellow undergrad at UCLA (pre-law).

Hunt Detective Agency

In-the-know Southland tongues have been wagging about Mimecom mega-honcho Tony Kreutzer and his latest up-and-coming Realitootsie, Miss Paige Katz. Here they are "cutting the grass" at a garden gala fundraiser for the PUENTE Learning Center at sometime mayoral hopeful and very Catholic power broker Richard Riordan's Brentwood home.

Paige
> The night you introduced us, he hit on me, heavily.

Harry
> I don't believe it. . .

Paige
> I thought he was just loaded and being funny — Harry's 'wild man' best friend. He was pretty out of control. A year later, you and I were fighting. You said some terrible things to me. Tommy came over. We got drunk. . .

Harry
> I'll wing the rest.
> (stung) The omniverous Paige Katz. . .

Paige
> It never happened again. When you and I broke up, Tommy thought I'd want to be with him — he became obsessed; even started working for the Senator, to be near me.

Harry
> Tommy worked for the Senator?

Paige
> (nods) Rose to First Tier, Synthiotics. They caught him trying to steal Mimecom software — broke the Senator's heart. That's when Tommy joined the Friends. (re: her betrayal) I'm sorry Harry.

[Note from Tommy Laszlo to Eli Levitt, attached to partial transcript of telephone conversation between Tony Kreutzer and Josie Ito, January 23, 1995. These documents were among those in the sealed files pertaining to the 1997 case of State of California v. Eli Levitt, made available in 2011 by the Fourth Amendment to the Freedom of Information Act.]

Eli —
   I thought you might find this transcript to be of interest. The "Fathers"-daughter relationship appears to be something of a weak link — any idea what this might mean? H.W. is a friend of mine. Could be a Friend? Please advise.
   — Tommy

Mimecom x326 Reel 3 (p.26)
(continued from p.25)
   JI: (cont.) was locked from the inside! He could have been in there all night. If you don't do something about it, I will.
   TK: Let it go, Jos.
   JI: She's my daughter! We're not talking about one of your Jonestown concubines —
   TK: If you mean Paige Katz —
   JI: Tony! Six months ago this wet puppy was dry-humping your girlfriend's leg — now I'm supposed to "let it go" when he starts sniffing after Grace? She's your niece, Tony.
   TK: And our boy is Dex Wyckoff's son.
   JI: He's a sap!
   TK: He's young. Believe me, he's got heart.
   JI: [Pause] Does he bleed?
   TK: I have plans for Harry. Don't be too hard on him. [laughter] And don't do anything that would leave him unfit for the duties of marriage.
   JI: It makes me sick.

   TK: [laughing] That's a good sign! I'm sure they'll be very happy.
   JI: They'd damn well better be.
   TK: Thatta girl! We'll dance at the wedding. I'll give her away.
   JI: It sounds like you already have. This better be on the up-and-up.
   TK: It's a family affair. Trust me, nothing could be better for Grace. I don't know about you, but I'd rest a lot easier knowing she's married into the fold, given that she's only half —
   JI: That's enough, Tony! I won't hear it.
   TK: I want this marriage to happen.
   JI: Don't threaten me!
   TK: Easy does it. I'm not questioning you. But it's a fact the girl is vulnerable. I just don't want anyone turning her head who —
   TK: Do you think I'm a fool?
   TK: No, but neither is [lost]
END REEL THREE

41

Can We Afford Channel Three?

The right of the American public to information was engraved in stone by the Founding Fathers. Today, lithography has long since been supplanted by digital phototypography, and the very phrase "engraved in stone" has but an antique charm. The words of the First Amendment, however, survive in any medium — as they must.

That Amendment guarantees access unfettered by government constraints. In practice, that most basic paradox: government regulation is required to guard against government interference. Hence the FCC — an electronic Coast Guard, if you will — patrols the airwaves to assure the fullest, freest expression of the ideas which ride upon those waves. The laws against monopoly, against cross-ownership, and against foreign ownership may be viewed as a constraint upon business, but they are fully necessary to avoid a constraint upon the public's right to know. It is in this context that the Attorney General is now attempting to block the sale of Channel 3.

The Attorney General — with, one can safely assume, the fullest support of the Administration — holds that he is trying to protect a vital national treasure from the ignominy, if not the threat, of foreign ownership. We believe the Attorney General is correct in his apprehension. Clearly, while the Wild Palms Group may or may not be foreign within the strict definition of the statute, it would be significantly more subject to pressure from various zaibatsu than are the American nets and syndies. And, as we have come to understand, the zaibatsu cannot be considered value-neutral with respect to American internal affairs.

The Attorney General also suggests that the Wild Palms Group is accountable to no one, that its clandestine tendrils, as has been widely alleged, extend far into *sub rosa* land. Might the Wild Palms Group use Channel 3 to advance the Synthiotics creed — or, more challengingly, the political ambitions of Mr. Kreutzer? In this apprehension, we must concur as well.

But those apprehensions, alas, are not the core issues in this matter. The fears of Attorney General Nofziger, however well-founded, are not sufficient to make national policy. What matters here, alpha and omega, are the rights of the American people.

In essence, the Administration here positions itself as a defender of the right to know, a defender of the First Amendment. It is hard to quibble with that Amendment. But it is possible to quibble, in this particular case, with the Administration's interpretation of the Amendment — which we find at best lopsided, and at worst tainted by self-interest.

Even the staunchest of Free Market advocates understand that monopolistic practices are not only bad for the public but bad for business. The growth in the communications industry, for example, following the breakup of Ma Bell, is but one example of the salutary effect of competition on once-sacrosanct sectors of the economy. Hence the Wild Palms Group's claim that it would bring new ideas — and a very healthy competition — to the inbred multicasting scene must be granted some credence. And the Group's contention that the threat of putatively foreign influence is less than the threat of stultification of the air- and cable-waves is similarly persuasive.

At the end of the day, it may be that the Administration is less troubled by the threat of foreign ownership, per se, than by the threat of "foreign" ideas. But while the Administration may not always see eye-to-eye with New Realism, it should not, cannot, ban an ideology, nor deny access to a movement.

The urge to protect a vital national resource is understandable. But that urge does not, in this instance, justify the full fervor of the Administration's efforts to block the sale. Perhaps the government is trying to enforce freedom *from* information — a right guaranteed neither in the First Amendment, nor anywhere else in our Bill of Rights.

We would suggest here a middle course. Let the Attorney General grant an interim license. Should the fears of the Administration — for which we may, perhaps, read the fears of Whittington, Kimble et. al. — be realized, then surely it would be no more difficult to decertify Channel 3's ownership that it was to challenge the Caltrans consortium.

The Attorney General asks, "Can we afford Channel 3?" meaning, of course, "we" the people. But we-the-people have another need here, equally pressing, equally guaranteed by the Founding Fathers: the need for diversity, the need for fresh air.

— From *The New York Times*, August 23, 1991

1.6. These texts are a book about the people and their Gods, or about the absence of Gods. Our hallucinations fail in attempting to comprehend and describe the Brains of Gods.

38.17. In any self re-Producing organisms there will be variations in genetic material. These differences in individuals will mean some individuals are more able than others to draw the right conclusions about themselves.

39.1. As God is actually a linguistic and televisual re-Production of the universe, then the Kreator is He who defines, describes, and makes a picture of IT in our own images. We are the Fathers and our goal is nothing less than to transmit a complete depiction of the "universe," and by this projection, to create an infinitely dense holographic picture, better than "reality," of what Synthiotics calls an Omniverse: a synthetic compression of light and matter in a curvature of space and time, being then quite certainly infinite.

45.5. The shorter the wavelength of Light, the more accurate our position as a Star in this Omniverse, and the higher the energy of each particle.

45.6. Each Father an uncertain principle.

47.8. If every Father is a Star, then Television is the Map that binds us.

85.2. The Mind informs the Brain. The Brain In-Forms its Self.

90.9. The Kreator understood that the Omniverse would finish up in such a high State of Order that it didn't matter what State it started in. In earliest times the Omniverse was in a Dis-Ordered State: No Garden. This would mean Dis-Order would decrease with Time. We do not see broken cups gathering themselves together and leaping back onto the table.

Dis-Order is intended to increase. This is a precept of the Fathers: Acceleration of Dis-Order.

104.8. SELF is the switch on your Neuro-Visual Screen.

123.23. The Fathers exist to direct the Weak-Force towards an Ordered State by any means or Media necessary.

123.35. Dis-Order in the Internal State is Insane.

123.36. Dis-Order in the External State is Outsane.

127.5. Memory and Omniverse have identical characteristics.

130.1. G.O. = General Order.

162.8. To see is to consume the Kreator, to be seen is to Father the Creation.

163.5. If Light is Matter, then Being does not Matter.

163.6. Being Light is another Matter.

163.9. Neuro-Visual Particles are the commercials that control the Mind. Once the Mind is controlled, we have infinite access for Synthiotic Brain programming.

201.2. The Soul of the Kreator becomes Immortal when He controls completely the Means of Perception. Seizure of the temporal State releases the energy of Order into the alternate State.

216.4. The Kreator is the Emissary of all Gods, the satellite freed from gravity, the wave of Light that travels beyond all Time. He is the Link with the Weak-Force. Their incarnation must suffer the last awe of Interference, their Signals must be jammed, their children stolen and their DNA neutralized, the Fathers of Order must access their Memories in a Final Program.

— Anton Kreutzer, *Confessions of a Go Master (1992)*

FROM: Frank Greenwell

TO: Josie Ito

Re: Polling results

DATE: June 8, 1994

Here are the initial results from our first round of polling, which we began last Thursday, immediately after our first media buy finished running. As the results clearly indicate, the ads have had dramatic impact; they may well end up constituting a benchmark in the history of political advertising. In short, *both* name recognition and general approval ratings for Tony have risen, *as have the total for the Fathers generally, and for the concept of New Realism generally.* The ads have struck a nerve — big time.

1. Are you familiar with the name Tony Kreutzer?

    May 5 *(prior to the start of the campaign)*

67% Yes	33% No	

    June 6 *(just after the campaign finished)*

80% Yes	20% No	

2. Do you have a positive or negative opinion about Tony Kreutzer?

5/5	42% Positive	27% Negative	31% Neither
6/6	56% Positive	24% Negative	20% Neither

3. Are you familiar with The Fathers?

5/5	46% Yes	30% No	24% Don't Know
6/6	59% Yes	24% No	17% Don't Know

4. Do you have a positive or negative opinion about The Fathers?

5/5	40% Positive	24% Negative	36% Neither
6/6	52% Positive	21% Negative	27% Neither

5. Agree or disagree: I support the philosophy and programs known as the New Realism.

5/5	22% Strongly Agree	28% Agree	10% Disagree
	14% Strongly Disagree		26% Don't Know
6/6	26% Strongly Agree	34% Agree	8% Disagree
	15% Strongly Disagree		17% Don't Know

As we discussed with you earlier, the totals for the previous three questions carry a higher degree of error than the others, given that those respondents ardently in opposition to The Fathers may try to disguise their feelings. Still, the degree of change is impressive, and may be generally regarded as an accurate measure of the change in public opinion.

6. Agree or disagree: I believe that under the present circumstances, we should allow the police greater leeway in the pursuit of their duties.

5/5	52% Agree	27% Disagree	21% Not Sure
6/6	64% Agree	24% Disagree	12% Not Sure

(The commercial with the dead young cop obviously hit home. The creative department guys and gals deserve a big pat on the back for that one!)

7. Normal constitutional protections should not apply to those suspected of nuclear terrorism.

5/5	41% Agree	39% Disagree	20% Not Sure
6/6	50% Agree	36% Disagree	14% Not Sure

8. I support Mr. Kreutzer's suggestion to fully implement Virtual Democracy by the year 2002.

5/5	49% Agree	28% Disagree	23% Not Sure
6/6	60% Agree (!)	24% Disagree	16% Not Sure

9. Agree or disagree: we need someone in the Senate who knows how to deal with the Japanese.

5/5	35% Agree	16% Disagree	49% No Opinion
6/6	51% Agree	12% Disagree	37% No Opinion

10. Agree or disagree: this country needs a return to spiritual values.

5/5	45% Agree	11% Disagree	44% No Opinion
6/6	58% Agree	9% Disagree	33% No Opinion

These results couldn't offer clearer guidelines about how to structure the next phase of the campaign, now scheduled to begin July 1. First, we need to keep stressing the issues that are hitting home, such as dealing with the Japanese and returning to spiritual values. Voters may not know who can deal with the Japanese or who has spiritual values. But because we're suggesting it, they're beginning to believe Tony is the one with

to
DISE

the experience to do it best. Similarly, the Virtual Democracy line is playing well, and we could get a lot of attention by test-driving the proposal and having Tony host a couple of electronic town meetings from Wild Palms before the election, maybe over the Labor Day weekend.

Second, we now have to begin handling Tony's negatives. Obviously if Tony gets portrayed as a "cult leader," then we've got troubles, only because we'll have to spend hours explaining that away. The way we handle this is by confronting the idea. If this sounds counterintuitive, like the idea of stopping your car from skidding by turning in the direction of the skid, well, it is. It is also equally effective.

First, there's a bunch of people who think Tony's a cult leader. We're never going to convince them otherwise, so forget 'em. For the others, we inoculate ourselves by compartmentalizing the things people find potentially disturbing, and then neutralizing them. There are three things which make people uneasy about Tony: first, his early writings; second, his relationship with Channel 3; and third, the synthiotics adoption program.

His writings: In the next phase of advertising, we're going to emphasize that Tony is a writer, a philosopher, and a spiritual leader. We will quote liberally from his writings as evidence of his vision and good heart. Steps should be taken to get his science fiction off the market and as far out of public view as we can. Of course some people will have copies and there will be quotes from the works that we don't like, so best to flood the market with the most palatable stuff.

His relationship to Channel 3: Quite simply, we portray him as a businessman and a leader. We tailor ads that surround him with characters from the various programs on Channel 3, which allows him to be associated with all the good times viewers have had watching the network.

The adoption program: This is obviously the most controversial element in the whole cult package, and we have to be careful to skirt the whole "kidnapping"

suggestion. I'm planning to do a long ad, in pseudo-documentary style, that shows some of the kids in the poor circumstances that they were in pre-adoption, and how much happier they are today. Then maybe we will show Tony picnicking with those kids and their families, playing softball or something (this could be arranged so as not to require more than a half-day of Tony's time), and thus associating him with all the love this program has inspired.

Finally, Tony's relationship with actress Kim Cattrall makes little difference to anyone. On the whole, Tony's negatives, compared with many successful candidates, are rather benign and highly fungible, so I'm not particularly worried, and neither should you be.

As planned, we will begin airing a series of Mimecom corporate image ads, which should make people feel even better about Tony. We thought your point about the jingle was right on, so Esai and Dick and the lyricist have gone back into the recording booth for another go-round. I am sure you will find their next effort a lot more "spiritual."

One concern: the preliminary polling for Mimecom is picking up certain problems we are going to be tracking very carefully before going on the air with the final version. We're finding that generally people like Mimecom, have warm feelings about the company, and trust the company to continue administering their medical costs. But frankly, they have funny feelings about Mimecom moving into education, basically because Mimecom is so deeply involved with the Perceptories. So I think a cosmetic change would probably be enough to allay their fears. With your permission, I'm going to test reaction to Educom and Mime-ed and maybe some other names. My guess is that people will feel better about some separation, even if it's a division within the same company.

FYI: one of our PR subsidiaries, Fletcher-D'Amico, was hired to publicize Tully Woiwode's next exhibit. They'll keep track of whatever's said.

NEW Cathedrals

My fellow Americans. . . . I address you as such because although I am running for Senator from California, this impending victory, which the polls assure me is about to be achieved, belongs not just to Tony Kreutzer, or to the voters of California, but to the American people.

It is 1994, and, I have achieved much in my life. I have written successful books. I have founded a great social and spiritual movement called Synthiotics. I have created a great corporation called Mimecom which has turned our savage and self-defeating trade war with the Japanese into a synergistic cooperative enterprise. I have begun the great task of freeing America from reality-control itself.

But I know I could have done none of it without you.

Without the thousands of workers and volunteers, without your faith in this great movement, there would be no Synthiotics. Without the skill of thousands of scientists and technicians, and without the talents of hundreds of entertainers, there would be no Mimecom, no Channel 3. Without your votes, I would not be on my way to Congress.

And without the support and protection of all you millions of people out there, who knows, I might be bankrupt, or in jail, or even dead. Because great enterprises attract vicious and unprincipled enemies, like the so-called "Friends," as surely as flies cannot help being drawn to fresh piles of steaming horse-dung. Without you, I would be naked on my own.

But what has been achieved is as nothing in the face of what remains to be done, in our State and for the Nation.

It wasn't chance or even climate that made the motion picture and TV industries evolve out here. And it's no accident that Mimecom started as a California dream.

California is where East meets West. Where West *is* East. Where the future begins. Where *realities* are created, where for almost a hundred years Hollywood has been the magic dream machine, the crown of creation, the unmoved mover, the void at the center of the Great Media Wheel: The New Jerusalem arising amidst the wild palms and shimmering mirages of the desert, the New Cathedral of our twenty-first century *self-made* reality.

But this campaign, this impending victory, is just the cornerstone of that New Cathedral. In the old days, when such mighty works were built of mortar and stone, it used to take centuries to build such an edifice, centuries of toil and dedication and faith on the part of generations who knew they would never live to see the fulfillment of the great dream.

But this is the twentieth century, my friends, almost the twenty-first, and these days things move a lot faster: at the speed of sound, at the speed of the electron, at the speed of the mind itself.

And while this New Cathedral will be a great spiritual edifice too, it will not be built of stone, but of light, and mind, and information, a communal structure we will all build and of which we will all be a part.

This new church, this great collective American enterprise, will not be bound by matter or time, for the New Cathedral will be a new reality entire. More, a multiplexity of realities. A new America to lead the world to a new tomorrow.

Together, we will build our New Cathedral. In our Father's house will be many mansions, and through the technology of Mimecom, each of us will get to decorate his very own. *E pluribus unum*, my fellow Americans. The One becomes the Many. The Many become the One.

[Excerpted from private texts that Kreutzer instructed the Fathers not to circulate, even with Synthiotics.]

The Guardians know that to take the victim and simply remove his suffering in the name of humanity, is to validate the weakness that first signalled his demise.

The Guardians have no illusions, for they are in themselves, ALL illusions.

The Guardians rule the regions of the unhinged Mind. They rule out sanity. Their people are those who have escaped blindness and chosen alternate realities denying preset values. They have delved into strange new areas of physical and psychic sensation, without the restraining limit of mental barriers. They have sought the deepest levels of sensuality, carried indulgence of the body and Brain to their limits and left the logic of the Mind and protection of the "Soul" behind. They have plunged together into consensual madness, have unhooked their receivers completely from the dictates of a "normal" Mind, followed an extra-terrestrial and extra-spiritual path that has neither judgment nor control for those who would travel and G.O. They rule the Mind-less cloud of lunacy, they pour water on the desert which is this world, they torture all certainty and master the pursuit of immortality. The Guardians seek to transcend the conflict of Mind, to rise beyond the boundaries of Brain to reach outside the limitation of Human values. They Will not sink into witless blindness but are aware, vibrant, and vision-satiated in the realm of Mindlessness, in the Space of hyperreal experience and immortal Dis-Order.

The Kreator can create and design realities, disorganize hallucinations, mold holograms into parables spinning life into Space, joining forces with the stars, leaving treasure maps to where true knowledge resides, hidden from no One. The Kreator can summon up infinite realities and access his people to them, he can generate and transmit every possible and impossible other-than-worldly vision, while those chains which bind Him to the earth fade into nothing slowly, leaving him to float free from the shackles of this Human Game above his world and into the puzzle and adventure of constant change and apparition destroying in finality all agreed-upon reality.

The Guardians will disconnect their terminal, their Brain from any social, moral, economic, or historical system, knowing in a most spiritual sense that the Enemy is Matter, and that until Matter is eliminated, the Soul is in bondage.

When the Mind is in confusion, the Soul is freed.

When the Soul is freed, the Brain attains weightlessness.

The Guardians will give us knowledge of all alternate realities. The Kreator will give us means and ends to worship and follow these realities, and the knowledge of the dis-Order that permeates them.

Mortality is the saddest reality.

Chickie

It's been twenty years since they broke my back and left me for dead. I had to lay under my mother's body, very still. Tell you why: after they killed her, they sat at the table and had dinner; ate the food she'd cooked just hours before. Even today, I can feel the weight of her. . .

Harry

You mentioned Mimecom — do you know the Senator?

Chickie

Our Father, Who art in Heaven, hollow be Thy name! The Senator wants a 'map to the stars' — don't we all!
You know, this burnt-out nightclub of a world doesn't thrill me in the least anymore. Soon I'll fade into the algorithm, won't I, Thomas?

WOIWODE ADOPTED HIM AND SENT HIM TO SCHOOL. CHICKIE TURNED OUT TO BE A COMPUTER GENIUS OF HISTORIC PROPORTIONS. HE WAS BUILDING VIRTUAL-REALITY SYSTEMS OFF IBM CLONES BEFORE THE TERM HAD EVEN BEEN COINED.

CHICKIE WAS OBSESSED WITH "THE SEA"— AWAY FROM IT HE LITERALLY BEGAN TO DIE. WOIWODE BOUGHT A LOT AT POINT DUME; HE WANTED TO BUILD CHICKIE A HOUSE, BUT HIS ADOPTED SON REFUSED. CHICKIE WANTED A SHACK, BUILT TO HIS SPECIFICATIONS.

NEARBY, BURIED DEEP IN THE OCEAN AND COOLED BY ITS WATERS, WERE THE MASSIVE "REALITY ENGINES" THAT FUELED CHICKIE'S CHURCH WINDOWS PROTOTYPES.

LiteSublime

By Deever Smith
[Reprinted from *Art Scene,* July 1995]

What could be more fitting than the State of California's decision to inaugurate its "Art in the Malls" program with a commission by Tully Woiwode? Woiwode's career, after all, has been marked by more fashion shifts than the garment industry, and his recent mural-sized abstractions — which look less like paintings than advertisements for them — could conceivably be interpreted as tributes to the cultural importance of shopping. The only problem is that this commission, following its current debut at the County Museum of Art, is slated to be installed in the Rodney King Mega-Mall. The selection of Woiwode has caused a minor scandal regrettable on at least two accounts: the committee's oversight in neglecting more politically sensitive artists, and the fact that Woiwode is in the limelight yet again.

The Sprawl, a one-hundred-foot-long canvas, is nothing more than a monumental doodle. With his usual cynical timing, Woiwode seems to have entered his "black" period: heavily applied charcoal-colored paint is webbed across the canvas in intricate structures, suggesting "both landscape and a vast written text," according to the show's catalogue, but in fact looking more like a Neo-Expressionist computer circuit board. It's lite sublime, the offspring of Jackson Pollack and diet Coke.

Woiwode, of course, has built a career out of convincing people that the lack of content in his art is the content. If there's no passion, intelligence or soul on display, it's because there's none left in contemporary life. "Individual sensibility has been dissolved in the electronic media puddle," Woiwode declares, and then goes on to paint from the viewpoint of the puddle.

And if the art doesn't look good over the sofa, clients know they can count on Woiwode to design matching upholstery. It's not for nothing that he's been called "the Merchant of Venice." Nor is it any secret that Woiwode's career has been boosted by influential friends and collectors in the reality-industrial complex. Current rumors link his State commission to lobbying by media mogul and Church of Synthiotics founder Tony Kreutzer, whose interest in Woiwode may have less to do with his painting than with the artist's close relationship with virtual-tech wiz Chickie Levitt — someone high on Kreutzer's corporate wish list.

A tireless promoter of his own historical significance, Woiwode's true art form is the fabrication and refinement of his celebrity persona. In his autobiography *Cancelled Reservations*, published at the ripe age of thirty-three, he devotes more space to discussing his movie star dinner dates than his artistic process. Judging from his comments in the catalogue, he's lost none of his talent for trivialization. "We live in a culture that has no memory," Woiwode maintains. "Likewise, I make paintings that have no memory."

Nor, fortunately, are they remotely memorable, except to the kind of Hollywood collector whose idea of early Modernism is Julian Schnabel. The one thing people will remember about *The Sprawl* is that a government agency once again failed to honor the cultural imperatives and needs of the community it supposedly serves.

REPORT   17F43U88 (if accessed)
DATE: February 20, 1996
TO: ORGDIR
VIA: DEPORGDIR
FROM: Chief, Investigative Services Division
SUBJECT: KREUTZER, Anton nmi, aka "Tony", wua. DPOB LA/CA, 6/8/41
SOURCES: ORGfiles, CIA, DIA, DepSTATE, DepCOMM, DepTREAS, DEA, SEC, NatlARCHIVES,
          Domestic Informants D 1-37; FonInfos F 1-42 (idens available), selected family members.

(This investigative background report is submitted per verborder ORGDIR and summarizes info sourced above
re captioned individual.)

SALIENT CHRONOLOGY:

Subject US Senator and presumed presidential aspirant, is the son of RAY KREUTZER and Miyoki LLEWELLYN, a half-Japanese, b. Kyoto o/a 9-19. d. 1945. Sister Josephine aka "Josie" b. 4-7-44. Early life in Bunker Hill sec of Los Angeles, details unknown. Delinquent recidivism 1957-62, allegedly due to Ray's death of alcoholism 6-21-57, and Subject's repressed knowledge of sister's and own long abuse by father. Sister (Josie) subsequently moved to Japan to be cared for and educated by mother's family.

1963: Subject begins successful career as writer of science fiction.

1967: Josie employed as translator USCON Kyoto; used access to obtain and relay info on Japanese culture and religion to Subject.

1968: Subject organized quasi-religious cult, Synthiotics, aka New Realism (q.v.).

1969: Subject befriends brilliant biochemist Dex WYCKOFF (indexed), an association leading to joint founding of Mimecom (q.v.). This umbrella corporation exploited WYCKOFF's work in pharmacology, neurophysiology, and artificial intelligence (specifics indexed) with enormous success.

FYI: Synthiotics and Mimecom benefited from state/federal patronage; in turn supplied product to sponsors: NASA, DoD, NIH, NIMH, HEW, BuPrisons, State LE agencies, RockInst, and selected univ medlabs specializing in psychresearch with biochemapps.

Subject gained popularity and enhanced public image through widespread sponsorship of drug-addiction street clinics, and media penetrations (in preparation for pol career). Clinics' role was recruitment for Synthiotics, testing/sale of Mimecom products. Concurrently Subject undertook sophisticated longrange campaign to subsidize/influence upper/midlevels govt/industrial leadership to ensure preeminence Mimecom/Synthiotics and insulate from challenge.

1975: WYCKOFF dies from self-administered gunshot wound, presumed accidental.

1978: Subject organizes Fathers, comprising members of media, church, military, USG, hi-tech corps, completely loyal to Subject. Fathers undertakes unattributable polacts including neutralizing polenems, smear campaigns, and sequestration of polenems' children in foster homes of fanatic Syntheists. Children taught to consider themselves American "samurai" adherents of Japanese bushido code. Latter reflects Japan-tropism of Subject and Josie, who married Japanese hi-tech industrialist Masaharu ITO ca. 1981.

1980: Subject begins pol career supported clandestinely by Fathers and their secret govt and media assets which provide inside info, advice, pro-Subject publicity, and antienem smear and rumor campaigns.

1983: ITO refuses to merge his industrial complex with Subject's. Eli LEVITT, alienated first husband of Josie, founds Friends as terrorist group dedicated to combating Fathers. However, Fathers and assets lodged within govt treat Friends as insurgency to be neutralized. (Pressure sources and domestic counterinsurgency techniques applied may merit special study.)

1984: ITO dies under mysterious circumstances. Josie takes control of his industrial complex, forming East-West axis with Subject. With Subject, she aggressively pursues media acquisitions/expansion, whose core is Wild Palms TV network. Subject's move to acquire Channel 3, contested by AG Nofziger, is ultimately successful.

1986: et seq: Subject's Wild Palms Group begins intensive mind-control research involving holography, perception-altering drugs and computer-generated neural simulations.

1994: Subject elected to Senate from California. Helps resolve trade war with Japan over digital TV technology.

1996: Subject's financial manipulations abet Depression which he attributes to current administration for pol gain.

SUMMARY:

Subject is a phenomenon unique in the history of this country. Unlike other industrial giants, Subject combines genius-level IQ with creativity, visionary prescience, amorality, a psyche conditioned and disciplined by Asian doctrines and religious traditions, and a passion for domination via non-traditional, clandestine methods. His brilliance in organizing the Fathers and manipulating their access at the highest levels of government and industry speaks for itself. Subject's control and exploitation of advanced technology and mind-control research merits close, continuous surveillance in view of his presumed Presidential ambitions. That Subject is guilty of heinous crimes is beyond debate although prosecution is not recommended, since it may be feasible to obtain for USG benefit exploitable aspects of Subject's hi-tech research, knowledge of intra-Japan industrial alignments, Japanese govt/media assets, pro-Japan lobby in US, Fathers' counter-insurgency org/techniques, and Subject's network of local level polassets/influence. The question to be ultimately resolved by higher authority is how to extract public benefit from Synthiotics, Mimecom and the Fathers without diluting their potential utility.

ORGDIR may want to consider covert enrollment of selected Fathers without Subject's knowledge; in that case a false-flag approach is suggested before other, more persuasive means are employed; among them, entrapment, bribery, prosecutorial threat, and defamatory publicity via cooperating outlets. Recruitment of disaffected family members is a parallel avenue worth exploration.

Privately, Subject has said, "What's good for Mimecom is good for America," which remark capsulizes his industrial and personal philosophy.

DEFINITIONS:

SYNTHIOTICS: *syncretic authoritarian cult whose initiates are taught awareness of "multiple realities". Members worship Subject founder and spread his vision of a New Realism.*
WILD PALMS GROUP: *conglomerate of reality-industrial media complexes controlled by Subject and providing a media power-base. Its mind-control research combines situational holography with empathogens, principally amazol.*

SUGGESTED COLLATERAL INVESTIGATIONS:

Josie; dtr Grace; ITO's industrial legacy; Harry II; murder of LEVITT's wife; assassinations and disappearances of Subject's enemies; identification of Fathers and their covert agents; relationships among Subject, Mimecom, and fongovs.

If investigative authorization granted, the foregoing listing is expected to amplify as relevant info is acquired.

. . .

nothing follows

51

TEAR AWAY

Men may stop a man from talking,
Break his legs & stop him walking,
Break his back & crawl & plead,
Make him scream & make him bleed,
Make him to renounce his creed,
Make him to obey.

You may not feed my brain synthetics,
You may not make me use prosthetics,
You may not give me amazine,
You may not make me dream your dreams,
You will not be a parasite,
Turn my daytime into night,
But you may pound it up your ass,
That would be alright!

Endless rules & regulations,
Bureaucrats that rape the nation,
Censorship that breeds frustration,
He will write a new equation,
O, such children you have made,
Blinded by frustrated rage,
Your example is disgrace,
You have taught them how to hate,
They will rise & take your place,
Violent, alien, lost in space,
The new psychotic human race,
They will turn on you one day,
And rip away your face.

You may not feed my brain synthetics,
You may not make me use prosthetics,
You may not give me amazine,
You may not make me dream your dreams,
You will not be a parasite,
Turn my daytime into night,
But you may pound it up your ass,
That would be alright!

[Originally recorded by Motörhead, 1997]

Woiwode
  The Depression this country went through was **planned**, Harry. And the Florida Bomb?
Gavin
  Ninety thousand dead —
Woiwode
  Know what one of our Southern senators called it?
Stitch
  A 'cotton burn-off' — controlled fire.

OCCASIONALLY I HAD A SMALL 'EPISODE' ACCOMPANIED BY MILD HALLUCINATIONS. MY DOCTOR CALLED THEM MISFIRINGS.

THE RESIDUAL VISIONS CAUSED ME ONLY BRIEF DISCOMFORT. FOR SOME REASON, THEY WERE USUALLY WAR-RELATED.

Woiwode
  No terrorists involved, Harry — strictly government. Boca Raton was a premeditated nuclear event that conferred extraordinary new powers on the police.
Stitch
  The Liberty Bell — textbook stuff.
Woiwode
  Within two years, the Friends were decimated — murdered or locked up in desert 'hospitals.'

A Small Circle of Friends
by P.G. McRoarke
[Reprinted from *Rolling Stone*, July 15, 1999.]

Not even in the chilly depths of the Marianas Trench could you expect to find a gang of creatures so resolutely ugly as the audience that gathered last week in Chicago at the World Friends Rally and Fundraiser. But the squadrons of fat girls with green hair and purple lipstick, the ectomorphic boys in their patched denim kilts — all of them with one eyebrow carefully shaved, perpetually giving them a look of being perplexed (say *wha*?) — were not unexpectedly disgusting. Malcontents of every era have worked hard to make themselves repulsive, at least to any but their own kind. Somehow they believe there's a direct relationship between maintaining a state of virtue and looking as though putrefaction was setting in.

Of course, sullen, ugly children weren't the only unsettling people in attendance. The usual gaggle of furry professorial types, fattened, hairless attorneys, and tall, homely literary women in the early stages of crone's disease were all in evident abundance. The highlights — and I use the term loosely, there being nothing at this event bearing a resemblance to driving down the Pacific Coast Highway in a vintage MG, with the top down and an attractive but not tiresomely verbal redhead in the passenger's seat — of the first night was the performance of the comedian Stitch Walken. (A clarification: this was a highlight for most in attendance. My personal highlight was finding the early nineties comedy *A League of Their Own* on the late show, and being able to catch a glimpse of one-time sensation Madonna Ciccione, before she ran to fat.)

Stitch was his customarily unfunny self. Carrying on about Tony Kreutzer and the New Realists would, you might think, provide a few chuckles (after all, the Senator pokes fun at himself often enough), and someone with a more acid sensibility might evoke some laughter, even if we all felt guilty about it afterwards. Instead, Walken, a wheezy and tic-besotted crank went on a "seig-heil"-laden rant, long on attitude, pathetically short on yucks. Well, maybe not so short. The foccaccia-faced scholars squatting before him laughed heartily enough. At what, though, wasn't clear.

Still, sitting through a thousand Stitch performances would have been preferable (after all, one could always hope to become punch-drunk silly) to the next day's dolorous discussion of the writings of Eli Levitt. Levitt — whom, you'll recall, is not Gandhi or Mandela, but in fact a nuclear terrorist — is currently receiving treatment for his screwball ideas in one of the country's more comfortable Perceptories. But this crowd would have you believe that this was an unkind fate for a mass murderer, and that Levitt should be released to find even more comfortable accommodations — say, at the White House.

I say harsher punishment should be exerted, not for blowing up half of Florida, but for his writing. Yikes! Levitt has perpetrated some of this old century's worst scrivening, accumulating clumps of clumsy prose so overheated that Thomas Paine by comparison looks like a diffident suburban schoolboy. Worse still, just when I thought the devoted had finished with Eli and I could go get a cigarette, they moved onto Levitt *fils* — Chickie, the boy genius of the Friends. He is now holed up somewhere, supposedly working on a new technology to counteract diabolical old Channel 3. If he's really a genius, he's down in Costa Rica with a couple of concubines, spending all the royalties he's earned from these nimrods, and working on his tan.

The one mildly entertaining moment in the weekend was a piece of agitprop theater that speculated some blow-up between Eli Levitt and Josie Ito. The notion gets points for imagination if nothing else, but

(continued on page 167)

A small case of mood poisoning; must be something I hate.

Tommy,

I write this letter as I might address a prayer to a god I don't quite believe in, uncertain you'll ever receive it — uncertain even that you're still alive — but hoping. Because that's all I've got now, just the hope that the person who has promised to get this to you is truly one of us and not a plant. That person claimed to be in touch with you already through the Friends, but then if he (or she) were a plant, he (or she) would claim that, wouldn't he (or she)? In any case, to avoid further pronoun problems in concealing his (or her) identity, should this letter fall into *their* dirty hands, I will say no more on that subject. And just hope this reaches you, as promised.

I could not be more miserable or better cared for. The daily bill of fare is a hospitalized version of nouvelle cuisine — bland but picturesque. Each morning I'm issued a new pair of pajamas that have been freshly washed, before I'm taken downstairs for the same thing to be done to my brain. I have not yet been physically tortured, though I've had the virtual reality administered more than once. Subjectively there's not much difference, except that once the amazol has worn off I find that my limbs, etc. are still intact, and all that remains of my agonies are the memories. And the predictable feelings: rage, terror, and a sometimes insupportable hopelessness.

The worst of it, at first, was having no idea why I'd been brought here, or what they wanted from me. Not information about the Friends, it seems. There were one or two *pro forma* interrogations, at which my interrogators were more concerned to show how much they already knew about us than to find out what I could tell them. And there was not much I *could* have told them. So I've had no opportunity for name-rank-and-serial-number heroics.

Their main purpose seems to be to convince me that I really am guilty of the crime for which I was framed. *They* know I could not be responsible for the Boca Raton disaster, since it was their brainchild (with a helping hint from Hitler and the designers of the Reichstag fire). *They* know that the 90,000 people killed by the Florida Bomb are 90,000 reasons *they* deserve lethal injections.

So they must also know that I cannot possibly believe myself to be guilty. Yet so boundless is tyranny's appetite for self-approbation that they will not be satisfied until their scapegoat, me, has repented for their crimes. When they've finally brainwashed me to their liking, will they then feel that justice has been satisfied? Or is it that all tyrants share Big Brother's need to control their victims' minds at the level of understanding that 2 + 2 = 4? Soviet "mental hospitals" in the heyday of the gulag were set up that way — field laboratories for testing out the potential for psychotropic drugs. The difference is that the Russians had only thorazine and the old hallucinogens, while the Fathers have amazol and the whole technology of virtual reality to play with.

In practical terms this has meant that each day I am led to "re-experience" my crime, as holographic simulations of my co-conspirators help me to assemble and deploy the suitcase bomb that destroyed Boca Raton.

Then there is a simulation of our "victory celebration" as we watch the televised coverage of the event that mesmerized the nation for the first weeks after the disaster. And then a restaging of the trial, both as it really happened and in an edited behind-the-scenes version in which Josie, my execrable ex, visits me (holographically) and implores me to confess my guilt — for my own sake and the country's good. What a bad actress she is! How I'd like to wring her holographic neck!

And yet. . . it gets to me. Even knowing everything she is saying is a complete fabrication, like her testimony at the trial, I am not always proof against the combined influence of the amazol and the television clips of the disaster. The ruined homes, the corpses floating in suburban swimming pools, the alligators scavenging the dead along the clogged highways of the evacuation route, the riots outside the hospitals, the looting and the increasing savagery of the police. I remember when I first saw those clips, before I was arrested, and realizing, as I watched a helmeted SWAT team plowing into a mob, that this was the reason for Boca Raton, that the whole thing had been staged to justify the consolidation of the ultimate Police State. That now and hereafter there would be curfews in *all* cities, *all* suburbs, even the smallest towns, that the horrors of Boca Raton would be the open sesame to horror as a way of life.

Then came the midnight knock on my door, and the interrogations, and the show trial with Josie's tearful testimony as its centerpiece. Already my memory has difficulty sorting out her original perjuries from the new improved versions I witness under the influence of

amazol. Is the entire world, I wonder, to be supplied with this revised version? It is, I must admit, more persuasive, more plausible, a better script. This version has been put together by professionals, and its quality is at least equal to the campaign ads of recent Senatorial candidates. They have the same knack for rewriting history to their own liking, and when the amazol is in me, I can believe it, even knowing all I know.

Tommy, I don't know how much longer my mind can withstand this new version of the Chinese water torture. Each day a few more drops of amazol erode the boundaries of reality a little more. My "therapists" urge me to accept my guilt as the only way of achieving true peace of mind. Write it all down, they tell me, for the story needs to be told so the country can be "brought back together." They have offered to bring in a ghost writer. How generous of them! But (I tell them) that would be unethical. I must write the story myself — in privacy, in circumstances that allow me to concentrate. And so I've been allowed this legal pad and a ballpoint pen, and I can come to this bench at the far end of the Perceptory's grounds, where it borders an abandoned air strip. A very private place and the likeliest staging point for any escape attempt. Please, Tommy, I don't know how much longer I can last. Don't let them redesign my mind as a weapon for *their* arsenal. Help me, I beg you.

Eli Levitt

Floating World
Los Angeles
1993 - 2008

[Excerpted from *Floating World*, by Ralph Rugoff and Fred Dewey.]

By the end of the millennium, it was clear to all but the most obtuse chroniclers that Los Angeles had emerged as the leading model of cyburbia. It was a Balkanized megalopolis which not only divided rich and poor as well as clean and dirty, but also drove a decisive wedge between mind and body, opening the way to the corporate colonization of private experience. These trends, though evident elsewhere in North America during this period, became the core of Los Angeles' new destiny.

Ironically, the paradigm emerged in full flower with the advent of the Ueberroth Plan, the last spurious attempt by the city's power bloc to create a more fully integrated metropolis. In response to the traumatic civic disturbances of April 1992, "Rebuild LA," a consortium of public and private agencies led by former baseball commissioner Peter Ueberroth, ostensibly set about rebuilding the crippled economy of South Central Los Angeles. As with similar efforts after the Watts Rebellion of '65, federal funds were pipelined into training programs, enterprise zones and development projects blessed by city tax breaks, while little was done to create long-term employment opportunities.

The centerpiece of the campaign, and its greatest embarrassment, was the construction of the Rodney King Mega-Mall at Florence and Normandie. Opened in late1994 as "the crown jewel in the city of malls," it was promoted as a site for local business, with a community center, a secured perimeter and an LAPD substation. The mall featured African-American motifs and a plaque commemorating the flashpoint of the 1992 uprising.

Neighborhood advocates weren't impressed. A year after opening, the mall remained only one-third occupied. The *LA Sentinel* mocked it as 'the Taj Mallhall', a symbol of the conspiracy to sell out South Central to "carpetbagging" by major real estate developers. Two years later it closed in the midst of the Nineties Depression. Bought out by the Church of Synthiotics, already known for its state-financed street clinics of the Seventies and Eighties, the Mall was eventually transformed into the Brandon Tartikoff Perceptory, an "experiential retraining institute for disaffected youth."

Tony Kreutzer, the man behind the Church, had purchased Channel 3 in the early 1990s, a move that thrust him into Hollywood's inner circle, and allowed him to play a behind-the-scenes role in another highly publicized component of "Rebuild LA." In 1993, Mike Ovitz, the much-feared power broker of Creative Artists Agency, had taken on the Crip and Blood streetgangs as pro-bono clients with the goal of merchandising Crip and Blood streetwear through the Gap. In the first year, "Peacewear" manufacturing plants in South Central churned out a line of customized b-boy hats, jewelry, red and blue bandannas, and stick-on tattoos. Rumor spread of a CAA campaign to have Ovitz nominated for the Congressional Medal of Honor. Within two years, however, as the Depression deepened and fashions changed, the enterprise went bankrupt and Ovitz mysteriously vanished, the rumored victim of a franchise turf war. Kreutzer stepped into the breach, enlisting ex-gang members through the Church of Synthiotics' aggressive neighborhood recruiting programs, which showed their first successes in South Central after the "Peacewear" fiasco.

With the derailing of the Ueberroth Plan, the Balkanization of LA was sealed in concrete by the collapse of Metro Rail, a multi-billion dollar subway system which went on line in early 1994. Greeted with the usual ballyhoo ("The city is finally accessible to one and all!" cheered Mayor Woo), the Metro Rail was plagued from the beginning by a combination of vandalism, violent crime, mechanical failures, and poorly located stations. With ridership low and the strapped city unable to continue its massive subsidies, service was cut back and in 1997 finally shut down by the infamous "Woo Decree." The transit tunnels, already filled with homeless, turned into an underground freeway for those on the wrong side of the law.

During the Depression, LA was not alone in its failed urban renewal, but the City of Dreams was especially hard-hit as jobs plummeted throughout the Nineties in aerospace, banking, insurance and tourist-related businesses. The sole bright spot was the concerted development of the electric vehicle industry. Though Metro Rail for a short while provided a market for rail consortiums, the new electric car had a more enduring impact. From initial test-marketing of neighborhood short-journey cars in 1995, to full-bore production in 1998 of the El Nino compacts, the industry took off, bringing jobs and clean technology to the LA basin. With smog levels dipping to pre-World War II levels, popular cafés were set up on overpasses, offering stunning views of the silent eco-friendly streams of traffic below. Exporting a line of retrofitted '60s-style sportscars, LA became the nation's eco-tech mecca.

As chief beneficiary of the new electric industry, Southern California Edison emerged as a major player in the reshaping of LA. Not content with its role as an economic and political powerhouse, Cal Edison pushed for a total ban on gas and oil usage. The company's notorious negative ad campaigns portrayed fossil fuel polluters as suspicious and vaguely criminal characters, who tended to smoke cigarettes and practice other "dirty" behaviors. "Keep America strong, clean and electric!" proclaimed billboards across the city. As many in the Latino and Black communities — those hardest hit by the Depression — were in no position to buy much of anything, let alone new cars, "Dirty driver"

became an epithet with racial overtones.

Cutbacks in public sanitation services reinforced the city's division into distinct "clean" and "dirty" zones. Those who could afford it hired private sanitation companies, while poorer neighborhoods did without. The fracturing of the city deepened in the late nineties with a radical real estate innovation: the integration of gated communities and theme malls. The latter had been pioneered in the early nineties with the European-style Two Rodeo Drive in Beverly Hills and Universal Studios' City Walk, a four-block simulation of "the essence of Los Angeles," replete with fake graffiti and dirty sidewalks. These car-accessible environments allowed consumers to shop in an ersatz urban milieu which was totally secure.

"Micro-cities" boasted similar theme malls with the addition of permanent housing. Zona Rosa, one of the first such developments, situated 4,000 dwelling units in "a sophisticated Mexico City environment" designed to appeal to an emerging Latino middle class. Once past the perimeter checkpoint, residents could safely enjoy a zocalo replete with restaurants, markets, entertainment centers and banking machines.

From the Westside to Hollywood and Burbank, micro-cities such as Seoul City, Little Kyoto and Park LaBrea II sprouted like the proverbial fungus after a rain. Hailed by the municipal report "LA 2010" as a breakthrough in creative urban planning, in practice these hermetic environments insulated their alienated residents, creating "communities" permanently cut off from each other and the city at large.

The popularity of the new micro-cities was in large part propelled by a rising fear of violent crime. LA had already distinguished itself as the world's bank robbery capital by as early as 1990, and in the decade that followed, assaults steadily escalated until banks were forced to close their doors to the public, switching over entirely to electronic transactions. Carjacking, another violent crime popularized in the early nineties, had reached epidemic proportions by the decade's end, leading middle- and upper-class commuters to hire minimum-wage, armed "driving companions."

The soaring crime rate, attributable to both the Depression and continued neglect of a growing underclass, was looked on by the City Fathers as a mixed blessing, since the booming security business was one of the city's few growth industries, swelling from an estimated 70,000 employees in the early nineties to approximately 200,000 by 2001. With their enhanced importance, Westec and other Japanese-owned security firms negotiated intimate links with the under staffed LAPD and Sheriff's Department. Besides sharing hi-tech surveillance and transport technologies, as well as mini-mall detention centers, the network of agencies collaborated to aggravate existing ethnic tensions as a means of keeping potential criminal cartels at war with each other — and away from secured areas. The dissolving line between public and private sectors — so characteristic of cyburbia — was epitomized by the rise of El Salvador-style vigilante groups, whose street actions were directed by a loose alliance of corporate and civic leaders popularly referred to as The Fathers.

Increasingly cut-off, the "dirty" areas of LA came to be collectively known as "Wilderzones." By the year 2004, this vast badlands — home to the city's poor as well as political outcasts — was over seventy percent Latino, and still suffering the poverty, isolation and police brutality previously cited as leading to both the Watts and '92 rebellions. Police abuses had been briefly curtailed in the mid-nineties by community videocam networks, but with the expansion of police powers following the nuclear terrorist attack in Boca Raton (1997) and the development of morphing and other video simulation techniques, the police regained the upper hand. This fact was dramatically underscored in the celebrated Serrano trial of 2005, in which a community video documenting the LAPD's fatal beating of Julio Serrano was pitted against a department version depicting Serrano making an unprovoked assault on LAPD officers. Faced with contradictory testimony from vid-tech experts as to which tape was "clean," the jury exonerated the officers, sparking what jaded TV commentators by then glibly referred to as "the usual riot."

In the aftermath of this "worst civil disturbance in American history," the city's policy of "controlled rioting" gradually crystalized, inspired in part by Hollywood's lead. On the heels of John Singleton's epic *Flames of Rage*, which won an Oscar for its "angry but optimistic vision," Universal opened Rageland, a holothemepark providing an "up close" experience of an urban uprising. According to a press release, visitors from South Central found it "a cathartic re-experience." Urban managers across the city saw an opportunity, hailing virtual technologies as the emollient needed to soothe the city's wounds.

From haphazard and rudimentary beginnings, the much-hyped creation of "virtual" electronic media grew into an organized industry of "reality manufacturing," the logical outcome of the merging paths of Hollywood and cyber-tech. The reality-industrial complex, a product of high-concept corporate mergers, began mass-producing consumer items such as the RB2 ("reality built for two") unit by the late nineties. Praised by civic boosters as "the last best hope for making neighbors of us all in the far flung city," virtual technologies in fact played a far more ambiguous role in reshaping LA.

Initial experiments seemed innocuous enough. Embracing "the bold continuum of news and entertainment," corporations like Mimecom and Times-Mirror/Disney opened popular holo-arcades featuring "reality programming." The latter conglomerate, after merging with McDonnell-Douglas, went on to transform the city's airport (sold off to refinance municipal

debts) into the Walt Disney International Traveland. A brief experiment with simulated travel for tourists of limited means proved to be a financial disaster, but the strategic importance of controlling the city's image at this key entry point was shrewdly exploited. Visitors were greeted by a network of constructed environments, imagery and service personnel, all painting Los Angeles as a stage set for Disney-style imagineering.

While virtual technology provided corporations with valuable communication tools, the new industry had a devastating impact on Hollywood's unions and guilds. It began innocently enough with the 1996 release of a new NC-17 rated *Citizen Kane* starring Madonna and Orson Welles, the industry's first "recombinant" film. When the first digitally-manufactured "stars" appeared on screen five years later, the Screen Actors Guild retaliated by leading an industry-wide strike. Citing the need to cut production costs, the studios — in a move applauded by Wall Street — responded by shifting entirely to virtual production. McDonnell-Times-Disney chairman Michael Eisner gleefully announced that "with three software programmers and our film library, I can create what used to take 200 craftspeople and three stars at $10 mil each."

Faced with declining prospects for a superseded and potentially unstable mid-level workforce, LA County opened the nation's first "Virtual Jobs" program. For life-long office workers suffering Post-Employment Stress Disorder, these interactive, "employment environments" provided cheap role therapy in the guise of simulated production tasks, staff meetings and regular opportunities for promotion. Meanwhile, the development of "virtual offices," backed by environmental groups as an energy-saving innovation and a means of cutting street traffic, further erased the line between corporate and private space. By the early 2000's, the term "home office" had taken on a new meaning, as the city's managerial classes found themselves sharing work-stations with their families. For the chronically immuno-deficient, a growing number of "virtual health" clinics sold a simulation of well-being. Taken together, these new technologies provided yet one more means for compartmentalizing and controlling the experience of the city's divided population.

For those trapped in the misery of Wilderzones and other low-income areas, there were few compensations for the virtualization of LA. Typically, the most significant contribution was a Japanese PR gesture intended to offset the effects of a decade-long, hi-tech trade war with the U.S. Toshiba Park, located in a drought-stricken area of drained pools and brown lawns, was the first holographic-TV park for the poor. Modeled on the early nineties Metro Park, a fenced-in municipal park designed to be seen but not entered, the one-acre Toshiba hologram offered stunning vistas of waterfalls, fields and lush forests. With the start of the black market in mimezine and other cathexis-stimulators in 2008, "going to the country" became the outlet-of-choice for masses trapped in squalor.

As a telling metaphor of life in cyburbia, it would be hard to surpass the opening in 2006 of the first Michael Jackson Immaculate Conception Clinic. An outgrowth of Jackson's charitable involvement in facial reconstruction for riot victims, the new clinic was devoted to the construction of perfect, virtual selves for the underprivileged. In practice, the center proved to be a laboratory where kinks in the technology could be ironed out using the underprivileged as guinea pigs. Along the way, countless youths, whose identity were already seriously fractured by socio-economic conditions, were subjected to experiments where their virtual selves disintegrated in uncontrolled morphing, producing permanent psychotic breakdowns. These unfortunate subjects came to be known, in local street parlance, as "jacksons."

February 4, 1997

An old woman froze to death in Malibu yesterday. I heard about it in the clinic when I took Coty in for his HIV vaccine. She was a squatter, it seems, living in one of those sheared-off houses on the Pacific Coast Highway. The nurse told me about it while she prepped Coty. "It's nice to know it still gets cold somewhere," she said with a mean laugh. Who knows whether to believe this kind of thing or not, with all the counterfeit newspapers being dumped on the streets. But it made me feel cruel even hearing the story.

I have a terrible confession to make: Harry and I are happy. It's our one subversive act, our little secret: we're the happy orphans, giggling and playing footsie 'neath the rockets' red glare. Too good to be true. I'm afraid it won't last. Sometimes I'm even afraid that happiness is going to scar me for life. I feel reckless, though — "drunk with love" — so who cares? You have to be pretty hard-boiled to be in love these days.

Josie came sweeping into the cottage this afternoon, all full of mystery and surprises. Harry wasn't home, thank God. He still doesn't trust Josie after she threatened to have him arrested for kidnapping when we came back from Las Vegas married. He'd never say so, but I think he respects her for it. Strangely enough, so do I.

She probably would have liked the wedding to be one of her coups, another episode of the Josie & Tony show. I called her from the chapel right before the ceremony and all she said was, "Remember who you are, Grace!" Meaning, remember who she is, of course. We both know *I'm* not much. No, I don't think mother ever really disapproved of Harry and me. If she had, well — I'd hate to finish that thought.

Anyway, this afternoon she bundled Coty and me into the Mercedes with great excitement, and off we went, winding up into the hills.

The upshot of it all is: the dear, wretched woman has bought us a house. Not just any house, a dream house.

That's just how she put it, too, standing there in the middle of the vast, empty living room, looking out at the empty pool (yes, pool!), Coty perched on her hip: "A house for my widdle Coty-woty baby-boo to dream in!"

And she meant it. The two of them are thick as thieves — I almost feel I should worry, but then when I see them huddled together, his white, dimpled hand resting on her leathery cheek, I get these sharp, gasping pains in my chest, pangs of hideous tenderness. Then I'm ashamed of my doubts — my jealousy, perhaps?

I told Mother I wanted to look around by myself, and then left them in the living room. There was something uncanny about the place, its deconstructed layout, all the oblique angles and unexpected curves — so hard to say just where one room turned into another. It felt like my real life. Secretly I was relieved. After growing up a mongrel princess in Japan, I am too used to being disoriented and out of place, an alien from birth. I always thought I hated Japan or that Japan hated me, but then just the other night I spoke to Harry in Japanese.

"*Doa-o akete kudosai*," I said, "Please close the door." He just looked at me like maybe I was an escapee from the VA hospital psych ward impersonating his wife. Then we laughed. (I think it aroused him because we made love that night.) I never realized that Harry hadn't known I could speak Japanese. I never meant to keep it a secret but — I wonder how many things about myself I've forgotten or omitted along the way.

What could I say to mother about the house? I said no, of course. I told her we were doing just fine in Echo Park. We could weather the Depression just like everyone else. We wanted to make it on our own. Besides, what would we do with all the candles, and the firewood, and the cannisters of cooking gas? She looked at me with a fierce, triumphant grin, and said, "Burn them!"

Coty squealed and clapped his hands in delight.

In short, I'm holding the keys in my hand. Harry should be home soon. . .

JUICE BAR:

Harry
It's these nightmares. . . I keep
dreaming of this — rhinoceros.
(He laughs.)

Tommy
Go on.

Harry
Only it's not like a dream, Tommy, not
even close. I walk into a room, and it's
there — real as this.

Tommy
I was reading an article — if it's any
help. Talked about schizophrenia as
an **allergy**—

Harry
Now I'm schizophrenic?

Tommy
Could be a diet thing.

Harry
(ironic) That's probably it. I'll just cut
back on cholestrol.

Tommy
The rhino: very sexual. The powder of
the horns — a heavy aphrodisiac.

Harry
(re: his impotence) That's a hoot.

Tommy
Have you seen a doctor? I mean, what
does your shrink say — what's his
name?

Harry
Schenkl. He says I'm about to learn
important childhood stuff — I'm
having some sort of breakthrough.

INT. WYCKOFF HOUSE —
KITCHEN — MORNING:

Harry
Is that decaf?

Grace
Did you want decaf, darling?

Harry
No, I'm fine. Hmmm — good foam.
You've got a real skill there.

Grace
You know I'm a damn household
goddess, Harry. Bagel's on the way.

Harry
What a night.

Grace
Remember your dream?

Harry
It was weird — I remember that much.

<u>Harry</u> (v.o.)
　　　The next few days were a blur. I was
　　　afraid to go to sleep at night. I kept
　　　seeing Schenkl, but he didn't have any
　　　answers.

Harry cautiously ENTERS the men's room
at work, with its foreboding stalls.

<u>Harry</u> (v.o.)
　　　I was even afraid to use the john at
　　　work; I didn't want to wind up with my
　　　pants down, next to that rhino.

Harry, at work, having heated words
with Marty Baum, a grotesque-looking
Attorney. Harry says something that
ends the argument; Baum looks at him
vengefully before EXITING.

<u>Harry</u> (v.o.)
　　　Work was bad enough. Marty Baum
　　　had been riding me for months about
　　　my "unaggressive caseload." Finally,
　　　I told him he was a corrupt, useless
　　　prick.

A ragged Harry sits at conference table
during meeting, about to doze off. Baum
keeps close watch.

<u>Harry</u> (v.o.)
　　　I knew Baum was the one who'd
　　　blocked my partnership — now that I
　　　was leaking blood, he was like a
　　　jackal, waiting for me to drop.
　　　Harry, as little boy, having
　　　Thanksgiving dinner in a modest home,
　　　with a modest family. He watches them
　　　bow their head and pray, then
　　　imitates, as if he's never done it.

<u>Harry</u> (v.o.)
　　　I started having flashbacks of when I
　　　was a kid. Foster family stuff I hadn't
　　　thought about in years — strange
　　　things, like being moved from place to
　　　place in the middle of the night.

Darkness. Harry, still young, being
hustled with suitcase into a van amid
flashlight beams.

Back in conference room, Harry
awakens from his daydream with a JOLT.
Baum and colleagues take note.

SISTER SOLDIER

The Grande Dame of New Realism Maintains a Touch of Fantasy at Home

by Slim Cutterpiece

"The fact is," Josie Ito was saying to me as she whisked out of her Miata 770Z and strode briskly to her front door, "the fact is, I hardly have any time for decorating anymore, and haven't for twenty years, since my brother went into politics." Then she swung open the door of her Isozaki-designed house in Bel Air to reveal an impeccably thought-out, beautifully realized Japanese interior. I stood for a moment soaking in the elegant, eclectic perfection of the space. "Well, you certainly didn't *believe* me, did you?" she laughed. "Come on in."

No, I hadn't believed her. Or rather, I believed her with the single reservation that I was fully prepared to believe exactly the opposite of anything she said within a moment's notice. But such is her charm. Josie Ito is an open and outspoken woman surrounded by sharp edges and silken traps. Of course, if you stopped to think about it, you probably wouldn't want anyone in so powerful a position to be any other way.

The paradox of Josie Ito is reflected boldly in her decor. The living room is dominated by a pair of six-leaf Japanese paper screens, six foot by twelve foot, depicting samurai in full battle

regalia. The exotically martial effect, however, is immediately undercut by a veritable gallery of cozy photographs of her grand-children — Coty, and his younger sister, Deirdre.

"Those kids are spectacular," Josie says. "You know, I *am* the best grandmother in the world." And she just might be, just as she is one of the world's leading connoisseurs of 19th-century Japanese art, as well as the savviest consumer of plastic surgery in California; the most articulate spokesperson for old Pa Mimecom on either side of the Pacific; and the sharpest, shrewdest mind in the stable of political wizards that has been corralled by her brother, California's maverick Senator.

"Is that a real rhino horn?" I asked, pointing to an enormous curved spar hanging above her fireplace. Below, on the mantelpiece, Josie had displayed her collection of spectacles, some antique, some brand-new and custom-made.

"Yeah, it's real," she said. "I'm a *hologram*, but it's real. Hey, do I touch everything in your house? Come on, I've got an early Woiwode I want to show you. It's so dreadful, I keep it around to remind myself of how bad a painting can get."

(Continued on page 336)

We signal and are signalled. We hold aloft a torch of fire and pass our hands across it. Visions, images, primal memories from this immeasurable Brain fills us with transmitted Light, dancing dots and lines, an end to the tyranny of language and a beginning of our return to the Garden.

— Anton Kreutzer, *Wild Psalms*

Paige
What about Chap Starfall?

The Senator
That's a hell of an idea. How is he?

Paige
We spoke a few months ago; he's going to be in town, on a gig.

The Senator
He did that old Sinatra tune I loved so much — what was it? (sings) Kings don't mean a thing — on the street of dreams!

Josie
Handsome boy.

The Senator
Lived out of garbage can on Zuma Beach. Crackhead — was one of those ATM bandits. Got probated to a Synthiotics house. Did damn well for himself.

Paige
He's a diehard New Realist — sober a long time now. Still does an occasional benefit for us.

The Senator
A fun kid. Why do I lose track of so many of my children?

Josie
Because you're a bizarre, self-obsessed old fool who coddles his enemies. . .

The Senator
(laughs)
Go and see him, Paige. Pull him in. Show him the wild blue sky.

SONG TO DADDY

I heard about you Daddy,
oh so long ago,
Never knew who you were
or where you could be seen.

Sometimes I wonder if you stopped
to think how cruel you've been
I need someone to phone home to,
I need someone to look up to.

Are you thinking about me now?
Are you? Are you? Tell me! Tell me!
Please!!

Or are you just a selfish personality
Somebody I seem quick to copy
Everytime I tell this story
I get so lonely, oh so lonely,
Daddy help me please!!!

You never write you just complain
You always joke and take great pains
To tell me how unbothered you are
About no one bothering about you

I know it's hard to care too much
When you're lost forgotten and out of
touch
But promise me you'll try to mean
much more
More than you ever did before
Are you thinking about me now!
Are you? Are you? Tell me, Tell me!
Please!!!

Your face is a pleasure
To read like a treasure
Lips like chapters
Lines to be whispered

I need your love to look up to
I need a mirror to see through to
You have this effect on me
You have this effect on me
Daddy help me please.

Are you thinking about me now
Are you thinking about me now
Everytime I tell this story
I get so lonely, oh so lonely
Daddy help me please.

FADE

YOU CAN CHANGE CHANNELS

Do you like the reality you are watching now? Do you like depression, bickering, poverty, war, disease, destruction? Do you like your self?
You can't change this reality. But, as the Buddhists say, there's more than one reality
And now **Dr. Tobias Schenkl's** Synthiotic techniques can help
switch *you* into these alternative realities.

THE REALITY YOU ARE IN

Half the people in this world are desperate to find a job, and the other half are being driven crazy by the jobs they have. 120,000,000 people die in an average year of wars, famine, disease and old age. Your days are filled with worries. Tomorrow your job could head south. Or your children could join the thousands who are missing.

But what a difference an "a" makes! It's the difference between being a worrier and a warrior.

TRAPPED BY LOW ENERGY?

This reality is not an illusion. The illusion is that it is the only reality. It is like being in Communist China, watching only one channel, and not having the faintest idea that there are lots of channels to watch — if only your tuner could pull them in.

You are trapped in this channel because all of your energy is focused on it. Without Synthiotics you can't turn your eyes to other realities because you are trying to feed yourself on the low-energy dreams of this reality. You are stuck in Channel 1. Only Synthiotics can provide you with the freedom to switch channels at will.

WANT TO SHOP TILL YOU DROP?

Your current reality is one of limitations. Limited cash in your pockets, limited credit. Limited time. Limited opportunities for jobs and promotions. Every move you make results in bills to be paid. The dishes always need washing and you are the maid. You worry all the time about your family and children.

Jump off the treadmill and experience The New Realism. Every move you make will become a dance through the illusory problem of life. You will find new opportunities. Your family will be safe and you can take them with you!

SOME BASICS OF SYNTHIOTICS

Energy is the substance of all realities. Each reality has a fundamental frequency — a channel. Human awareness is a configuration of energy that can be tuned to any of the different frequencies. But when conscious energy is low, you can get stuck in a single channel.

Shamans, men of knowledge throughout the ages, knew these secrets. They were able to channel some of the different realities and use that knowledge to help in this reality. But society has traumatized most people so that they can only tune into one frequency — Channel 1.

Quantum Physics is the rediscovery of the true principles of energy. It has made transistors, lasers and holograms possible, and with these instruments techno-shaman and Synthiotics founder Tony Kreutzer has developed techniques to help you access the higher channels.

Holograms aren't just three-dimensional illusions. Reality is a hologram — that is why you can walk through it. Every part of it, including you, contains the whole. When a part goes, everything must go. You already contain all Channels. Everyone is switching to The New Realities. Don't be left behind.

Immortality is achievable. Death is Channel 0 — it's what happens when you don't even have the energy to stay tuned in

TO THE NEW REALITIES

Channel 1. Synthiotics is a technique for gathering and using human energy. Learn to conquer the countries of your imagination, one by one, and join Tony Kreutzer's dream into infinity.

Everyone must Go. You can go to Channel 0, or you can go to The New Realism. The Choice is yours.

CLASSES AVAILABLE

Finding the On Switch

Synthiotics introductory class. You'll receive your first training in refocusing your mental energies. You'll be introduced to Mimecom's Tools for Synthiotic Discovery, devices that help you shift your mind out of Channel 1. See the difference in yourself for yourself!

Changing Channels

Serious training in switching between Realities. How to assemble and deploy your mental energy. Getting a clear picture. Become a power viewer — someone who decides which shows get aired. Join other Synthiotics adepts in the new realities!

Becoming a Star

Watching is only half the fun! You can be a star, an actor on the stage of life. With Synthiotics training you can rehearse a leading role, interact with other stars, and gather charisma, the magic energy that inspires allegiance and devotion. When people admire you they will go out of their way to help you. Why just gaze at the stars when you can take your place among them?

WHO IS TONY KREUTZER?

Tony Kreutzer, the founder of Synthiotics, is a true American success story. His father was a minister; both his parents died when he was young, leaving him an orphan. Yet he went on to become a best-selling novelist and the inventor of over thirty patented devices. By the age of thirty-five he was a millionaire; by the age of fifty he was a billionaire. And he still is!

These devices, based on quantum physical principles, enabled him to begin exploring alternative realities. He's the trailblazer for Synthiotics, the Daniel Boone of the New Realism. Over fifty million people worldwide have read at least one of his books; over five million have taken a Synthiotics course.

Tony Kreutzer wants to share his discoveries with you. He wants you to join him in storming heaven. Channel 1 is losing the ratings battle. Get ready to blast off! Tony is the Captain who wants to leave this reality with a full crew on his ship. Don't be left behind!

Come to a free seminar with
Dr. Tobias Schenkl on
THE NEW REALISM:
SYNTHIOTICS
Thursdays and Sundays 7 P.M.
1095 Market Street, San Francisco

To: Jules Sapanara, Research Division, Palo Alto, CA
Mimecom Corp.

From: Dr. Peter Caraway, Upper Midwest PHARM, USA

As of April 2006, we have reason to be even more optimistic about both our street-clinic and interactive technology programs. What follows has applications not only for synthiotic therapeutic techniques, but, eventually and potentially, for entertainment and games on CD, 3-D television, and so forth.

Building on our success with choline and phenylalanine precursors, we are taking the next step from smart drugs and memory drugs to *smart memory* drugs.

The S-M Formulation, as it is known around here, works in two steps: 1) primary activation of the amygdala and hippocampus for memory enhancement, and 2) secondary activation of pons neurons in the brain stem, in conjunction with temporal lobe stimulation, to produce *interactive memory.*

Which is to say, a programmable memory the individual can interact with as a form of reality, rather than just experience as an especially vivid "mind movie" — which is how most people experience both memories and dreams.

There are, however, certain members of the population who are capable of *lucid*, or *interactive* dreams — i.e., during the dream, the individual recognizes being in a dream state and seizes control of the action. We have studied these individuals, awake and in the REM stage of sleep, seeking to discover what differences in brain chemistry could account for this fascinating ability.

We found our answer and, after several experiments involving hypnotics and trance-drugs, created the S-M Formulation. One key was recognizing the transition between passive dreaming and active dreaming, and tying that in with the active (rather than passive) experience of *remembering*. Remembering is voluntary, which is to say, the individual chooses to remember an incident, a person, and so forth. But once the memory is triggered, the individual goes from an active mode to a passive one. We wanted to keep the individual in an active state vis-a-vis content and outcome.

The other key was engaging all memory, rather than just part: prior to the S-M Formulation, we had been concentrating strictly on cognitive, or informational, memory — objects, places, people, dates. But we had completely neglected *non-cognitive* memory, which is sometimes called the "memory-less" or non-verbal memory, and which reconstructs processes and procedures — e.g., you know how once you learn how to ride a bicycle, you never forget? This is why.

As soon as we dealt with *whole* memory rather than just the informational part, we were on our way. We prepped our subjects by easing them into a trance state, so that absolutely no stimuli from the outside world could interfere or distract. Then we administered the S-M Formulation through a slow intravenous drip to the carotid.

The S-M Formulation works in two stages: in the first stage, it activates the cognitive memory through the temporal lobes, and then releases chemical tracers throughout the brain which stimulate and activate the non-cognitive memory associated with the particular incident being remembered. For example, if a subject is remembering a walk in the park, the S-M Formulation activates the non-cognitive memory of how the legs and arms move, how balance is maintained, adjustments in breathing, and so forth.

In the second stage, the pontine neurons are stimulated to secrete acetylcholine but also, at the same time, to produce norepinephrine, which will suppress the REM state — we want the subjects' brains to draw solely on their memory without entering the dream state. In other words, we set them up to dream, but instead, they get an enhanced memory.

After two or three sessions with S-M, the subjects

grow accustomed to this new state of mind and become able to run sequences of events two, even three times in a row with no loss of focus and, more importantly, with no incidental drift (i.e., no deviation from events as initially remembered). They then interact with the memories as if they were dreaming lucidly, which is to say, they re-enact and/or relive the memories, *but they make whatever changes they — or we — want in the sequence of events*.

Typically, it works this way: a "memory-naut" will first go through the recalled sequence in a passive mode, as if watching television, interacting only enough to mark critical points with a virtual placeholder (the equivalent of a bookmark). In order to keep each point clearly marked, the same image was given to every subject for placeholding use: a cathedral. The cathedral image is very small until the memory-naut finds the right place (or places) to put each one; then the image expands to fill the available memory-space. To engage in "lucid remembering" — i.e., affecting the sequence and outcome of the memory — the memory-naut enters the cathedral on the second (or third) time through, encounters a television set, and turns it on. This television is actually an interactive device, which allows the memory-naut to alter that portion of the remembered sequence by manipulating the images on the screen. This sort of "storyboarding" enables the memory-naut to test each proposed alteration. If the outcome is not desirable, the memory-naut "rewinds" and starts over. Eventually, we may have subjects who are able to effect rewind during interaction.

Our best example of results: one subject successfully ended a drug addiction of many years' standing by rewriting his memory in such a way that he never accepted a first dose of the addicting substance. Subsequent scans confirm that receptors for the drug formerly present in the subject's brain no longer exist. The subject effected not only a cure but a retroactive cure. While certain other physical effects — heart, lung, and liver damage, for example — were not reversible, the cure stands as our most positive development. "If I knew then what I know now" is not necessarily moot any more. Those able to heal certain events of their pasts as definitively as this subject did will be in the vanguard of new, more effective treatments.

So far we have not forced the issue of restricting or directing the course of changes made, but as you can see, the potential is — well, practically unlimited. We have taken the first step toward our ultimate goal of reality manipulation. Whatever we want to use this for, we can use it for — and so can anyone else. So I suggest we keep security very tight around this one. Can you imagine what would happen if some company unfriendly to us or our cause got hold of this?

As far as Synthiotics goes, I'd say the sky was the limit, but I think it's even more wide open than that.

[Jules: when you reformat this for submission, please do NOT include the report on Subject B's re-addiction and re-cure. Since these are convicts, there is nothing to be gained by showing B's self-indulgent behavior. Normal people would not take the attitude that "it's OK to get hooked again because I can be cured any time I want to" (but even if they did, we could fix that anyway). DO include my notes re the "healing the inner child" therapies so popular in the late eighties and early nineties. Now the "inner child" has an "inner Big Brother," so to speak, and if we can get more funding, we can keep "inner Big Brother" turned on constantly. Hell, we might even heal everybody's inner child and then move on to regression therapy and heal the inner child's previous lives.

Just kidding about the previous lives, Jules, don't put that in.]

Thx, PC

We should like to be able to convey an impression of the dazzle and vertigo produced by these immobile Byzantine people; the fixed eyes turn; the arms, of Egyptian gesture, move; the fixed feet begin to walk; the cherubim wheel upon their eight wings; the angels spread their long feathers of azure and purple nailed to the wall by the implacable mosaist; the genealogical tree shakes its leaves of green marble; the lion of St. Mark rises, yawns and stretches out his clawed paw; the eagle sharpens his beak and plumes his feathers; the ox turns on his litter and ruminates as he swings his tail. The martyrs arise from their grills, or get off their crosses. The prophets converse with the evangelists. The doctors make observations to the young saints, who smile with their porphyry lips. The people of the mosaics become processions of phantoms that go up and down the walls, circulate the galleries, and pass before you shaking the hairy gold of their nimbuses. It is all dazzle, vertigo and hallucination!

–Théophile Gautier,
Famous Cathedrals

Harry
Gavin, what is this?
Gavin
The Mimezine — it's flooding your cerebral cortex!
Beauty Queen
(moving closer) I saw the way you looked at me onstage. I wanted you to touch me...

Harry laughs nervously — he doesn't quite believe what he's experiencing.

Gavin
Go ahead! The adaptor's tracking your hands — the mimezine'll give you the illusion of touch.

Harry slowly extends his hand and 'caresses' her cheek. The Beauty Queen sighs, and puts her hand atop Harry's; he clearly feels something there.

Beauty Queen
You made me queen of the pageant; now I'll make you king...with my mouth.
Gavin
Go for it, Harry!

She leans to him, kissing him on the lips.

Gavin
Yes! Yes! We have contact! Yes!

INT. WYCKOFF HOUSE —
BATHROOM — NIGHT:
Harry, still in shirt and tie, sits across from Grace as she soaks in tub. Only a candle glows.

Harry
It was the weirdest thing I've ever experienced...
Grace
Was it legal, what he gave you?
Harry
Mimezine? It's not even classified yet. Works on the lower brain — the reticular something-something. They're tapping into some kind of primordial, cortical weirdness — what they've been talking about is true, Grace: it is a new reality...
Grace
Hail, Synthiotics!

THE PHARMACOLOGY OF MIMEZINE

THE MURCK MANUAL 14th Edition

9179. Mimezine. 4-methoxy—[b—(3,4-methylene-doxy-2-vinyl-*(benzyl)-octahydro-12*-*(hydroxymethyli-mino)-5,9;7,10aH-[1,3]dioxoamidine* - *4,7,10,11,12-pentol*, mimaspherodine; kavatetrondon; taricha-kavatin; MDTX. $C_{26}H_{31}N_3O_{10}$. mol. wt. 593.28. C 52.59%, H 5.23%, N 7.08%, O 35.06%. Semi-synthetic derivative of the toxin from the ovaries and liver of many species of *Tarichadontidae*, esp. the globe fish (*Spheroides rubripes*), Yaka. *J. Chem. Soc. Japan 71, 590* (1950). The methelenedioxy side-chain similar to that of kavatin, the principle ingredient of the root of the tropical shrub, *Piper methysticum L.*, (kava). Original synthesis: Mimecom, unpublished (2007). Modern synthesis abd pharmacology Narahashi, *Fortschr. Chem Org. Naturst. 22, 266*, (1998). Mechanism of action, Kao and Fuhrman, *J. Pharmacol. Exptl. Therap. 387, 102*, (2002). Spectroscopic and chromatographic studies of mimezine, its metabolites, and its acid hydrolysis products: Lafarge et. al. *J. Anal. Tox. 168, 23*, (2005).

Darkens above 220 without dec. [∂]29-8.6. pKa: 8.76 water; 9.5 (50% alc., ether). sol in dilute acetic acid; slightly sol in water, dry alc, ether; practically insol in other organic solvents. Degrades upon stainding in acids and in alkaline sols. LD50 i.p. in mice 15 mg/kg. Pandey and Rinehart *J. Pharm. Appl. Tox. 247, 831*, (1997).

Research into mimezine synthesis was originally begun in 1969 by D. Wyckoff, but was not published in the scientific literature. It is thought that mimezine was the result of a clandestine research program focused on the preparation of semi-synthetic derivatives of tetrodotoxin which would have greater psychoactive properties. The isolation and tentative identification of tetrodotoxin was accomplished in 1963 by Buchwald et. al. *Science 368, 771* (1963). Structural confirmation and total synthesis of the tetrodotoxin followed a joint U.S.-Japanese collaboration. Tsuda et. al. *Chem. Pharm. Bull. 12, 157* (1964).

The effects of tetrodotoxin on the peripheral nervous system have been known since earliest times. Pharmacological studies of the toxin demonstrated that it acts by blocking the conduction of electrical signals along both sensory and motor nerves. Tetrodotoxin concentrates in the ovaries and testes of the puffer fish (*J. Fugu*). Poisoning, resulting from the eating of these parts of the puffer fish, is characterized by numbness and tingling, followed by a gradually increasing weakness of all muscles. Death results from the total paralysis of respiratory muscles.

Low doses of fugu toxin produce a paradoxically enhanced sense of tactile perception which may be perceived as having sensual or erotic overtones. This is thought to be due to the "inhibition" of inhibitory tone of the skin. [Note — Without this "inhibitory tone" the wearing of clothes, gentle touching of the skin, or any small change in skin temperature would be perceived as extraordinarily distracting, even painful.]

By coupling tetrodotoxin to kavatin, the active principle of the Kava plant, Wyckoff attempted to decrease the toxicity of tetrodotoxin and enhance its psychoactive properties. Kava is a natural product with a long history of ritual use in the Fiji and Tonga Islands. Its structure, interestingly enough, is similar to that of methylenedioxymethamphetamine (MDMA, ecstasy). Hence it is not surprising that it has been used ritually at tribal gatherings to facilitate social harmony and communication. Kavatin was studied extensively by pharmaceutical companies in the fifties for potential use as a therapeutic agent. However, the itching and flaking of the skin which results from its chronic use caused these studies to be abandoned.

Mimecom's success in fusing tetrodotoxin to kavatin resulted in a drug with unique pharmacological properties. Low doses of mimezine produce what might best be characterized as highly enhanced tactile sensations which have been described as "aphrodesiac-like." Higher doses produce more extraordinary and unusual sensations, which may be equivalent to "tactile hallucinations." That is, the drug produces sensations not normally experienced. One common experience reported is synaesthesia, i.e. the blending of tactile sensations resulting in "colored warmth," and/or the sensation of "light touch coupled with a low rumbling sound."

The mechanism of action of mimezine has not been fully elucidated. However, it appears to work primarily at the level of the spinal cord. More recent work suggests that some primitive structures of the brain may also be involved. It is thought that mimezine inhibits the "gating" mechanism of the spinal cord, the mechanism that regulates the transmission of sensory information to the brain. Normally the "gate" allows only vital sensory information to be transmitted to the brain, such as position of the limbs and skin temperature. Mimezine's inhibition of the gate causes all sensory input to be greatly enhanced, often with a fusion or multiplexing of sensations. The World Health Organization's Committee on Dangerous Drugs and the U.S. Drug Enforcement Administration had originally classified mimezine as a hallucinogen with potentially addicting and dangerous properties of no medical value (Schedule 1), but subsequent testing by the Food and Drug Administration resulted in a license being granted to Mimecom for manufacture and distribution. Early applications included treatment for trauma, depression, and prosthetic therapy, often in conjunction with holographic and/or interactive visual programming.

seeing is
Bereaving
feeling is
Reliving
touching is
Relieving!

Loss — real or imagined — is a pressure point of life that very often gives rise to depression, anxiety, and a generalized rejection of pleasurable activities. In cases where the patient sees no end to grief, loss can generate a cycle of depressive symptoms that threaten the successful completion of the grieving process. In such cases, a combination of **Mimezine** and holotherapy can bring the patient back from the brink of hopelessness.

The empathogenic and synaesthesic properties of **Mimezine,** administered to the patient in conjunction with exposure to a flawlessly accurate holographic simulation of the lost loved one, enable the "couple" to once again share tender moments. The grip of depression is broken as hologram, psychoactive agent, and sense-memory fuse, and the patient once again experiences the sensation of having something to live for. Once the depressive cycle is broken, therapy may be tapered slowly until the patient's sense of well-being and independence is restored.

When administered under a physician's care, **Mimezine:**
• is non-habit-forming
• rarely overstimulates
• helps assure a good night's sleep.

Back "in touch" with life. . .
Mimezine®
(mimaspherodine)

MimeCare

Please turn page for brief summary of prescribing information

Paige

Tony thinks our world's a dream; a miserable one. In our unfathomable arrogance, we call it the only game in town — 'reality.' Chickie felt the same way: that the universe is all energy, dreams within dreams. Chickie and the Senator loved talking about a ghostly place — the place where holograms go when you turn off the TV. Beyond the Net. . .

Harry

And through the 'Church Windows'! What about the thing in my hand?

Paige

A bio-chip — a computer that crunches molecules instead of numbers. Chickie called it a trapeze for the Senator's soul; something to grab onto when he flies into space —

Dreams are the coded material of eternity. We possess LIGHT through them.

He who controls LIGHT controls mortality.
He who controls LIGHT controls immortality.

Nothing matters but the end of matter.

— Anton Kreutzer, *Wild Psalms*

73

EMAIL text archive, Kyoto University datacenter, December 2010
Date: Tuesday, 9 February 2006, 3:27 UT
To: Chickie Levitt <chickie@neuro.usc.edu>
From: Ushio Kawabata <ushio@kyotou.jp>
Translation: jpl->aml
Encoding: text:rsa-pubkey

Your musings yesterday on a permanent broadband mental link to the worldnet were very thought-provoking. I think you are right: it would allow the human mind to bootstrap itself in an effective way into an entirely new, and much larger, arena of possibilities. In the early stages the effect would be of an expanded mind, with the contents of the world libraries as accessible as one's own memories, and the computational capacities of the world's computers as available as one's own skills. As integration proceeded, one might slowly download one's entire personality into the net, being thus freed from all limitations of the body. It is hard, from our present standpoint, to even imagine what might be seen and reached from that perspective.

Have you any ideas on how to proceed? There was an article yesterday article in *Comp. Par.* on Andrew Systems' Crystal 3. It is probably powerful and small enough to serve as a data compressor for a link: only 1/20 cubic meter for 10 TeraOps: Perhaps one could carry it in a backpack for a perpetual connection?

****

Senator

Chickie Levitt's a legless little liar! He's holding out on me: a fiasco of red herrings. They're alchemists, Paige! Ushio and his forty-seven Ronin! You know what 'infinity' is for them! A cologne you dab behind the ears! It's that easy — they know what to do with the memories of old men —

Date: Tuesday, 9 February 2006, 8:16 UT
To: Ushio Kawabata <ushio@kyotou.jp>
From: Chickie Levitt <chickie@neuro.usc.edu>
Translation: aml->jpl
Encoding: text:rsa-pubkey

Ushio-samba!

Well, it would still give a pain to carry your brain. A backpack compressor might offer higher bandwidth to the net, but would be much less convenient than a straightforward Eiglass optic nerve interface (and considerably more risky). I've been thinking of a way around having to put all the processing in electronics, and still get higher overall bandwidth in a vastly more compact form. *If* we could get the neural connections to cooperate — to crossbar and compress the calloflow — we could save 99% of the computation and external communication, making callosum interface practical — with data rate low enough for a sat-cell relay. So then, you would have to carry around only a standard multiplexer and sat-cell transceiver. The hard parts of the operation can be distributed anywhere over the worldnet!

****

Date: Tuesday, 9 February 2006, 8:48 UT
To: Chickie Levitt <chickie@neuro.usc.edu>
From: Ushio Kawabata <ushio@kyotou.jp>
Translation: jpl->aml
Encoding: text:rsa-pubkey

That would be artful – a few chips at your end, giving access to the world's data and processing power. Not only images and sounds, as with Eiglasses, but with callosum access, feelings, motor sensations and more abstract mental concepts, since the connection is to your cortical areas for those functions. One could be in touch with almost anything in the web with an intimacy now possible only with one's own thoughts! (On the other hand, there is a danger from useless net blabber all day long, like mental tunes that will not cease).

Small problem: The crux of your suggestion lies in building biological neural structures that do most of the job we have been trying to do with electronics. How does one persuade the neurons to, so conveniently, arrange themselves to compress your callosum flow for satellite transmission?

****

Date: Tuesday, 9 February 2006, 9:15 UT
To: Ushio Kawabata <ushio@kyotou.jp>
From: Chickie Levitt <chickie@neuro.usc.edu>
Translation: aml->jpl
Encoding: text:rsa-pubkey

Well, that's the hard part all right. I have been reading about gene hacking in sci.bio.research by the nerve repair crowd at Hopkins. They've managed to develop viral vectors that infect neurons and bugger their genetic initiator sequences, so neural stem cells begin differentiating in mid-growth. They can grow an isolated callosum. The ends come out tangled, since there's no place for them to connect to.

* * * * * * * * * * * * * * * * * *

Date: Tuesday, 9 February 2006, 9:34 UT
To: Chickie Levitt <chickie@neuro.usc.edu>
From: Ushio Kawabata <ushio@kyotou.jp>
Translation: jpl->aml
Encoding: text:rsa-pubkey

There must be many difficulties there. My friend Toshi Okada, who does gene-engineering at Tskuba, tells me that in embryology, almost half the information required to properly grow cell structures comes from the previously grown structure: expressing the DNA code alone is not sufficient to build working assemblies in most instances. Perhaps additional coding could be added to substitute for insufficient external framework? It would be like building scaffolding in preparation for construction proper.

* * * * * * * * * * * * * * * * * * *

CHICKIE STARTED TO TALK. I FOCUSED ON HIS MOUTH TO EASE THE VERTIGO.

DID YOU KNOW THAT IN ROMANIA—TRANSYLVANIA—WHEN YOUNG WOMEN DIE BEFORE MARRIAGE, THEY MAKE THEM BRIDES AT THEIR OWN FUNERALS?

OH, YES—THEY HAVE THE CEREMONY RIGHT AT HOME. THE BRIDE'S ATTENDED BY FAMILY AND FRIENDS AND A BRIDESMAID IN A LAVISH GOWN.

ONE OF THE VILLAGE BOYS STANDS BESIDE THE COFFIN, RECITING THE WEDDING VOWS; THERE'S EVEN A PRIEST. IN THE BRIDE'S FOLDED ARMS IS A SMALL DOLL.

THE DOLL SYMBOLIZES THE CHILDREN SHE'LL NEVER HAVE. THEY CALL IT "NUNTA MORTULUI"—WEDDING OF THE DEAD.

THE WHOLE TIME CHICKIE SPOKE, I WAS AWARE OF A PRESENCE COMING TOWARD US. I TURNED MY HEAD AND SAW HER—A THIN BLACK BALLERINA.

CHICKIE INTRODUCED HER AS TERRA, HIS FIANCÉE. HE SAID SHE WAS JOINING US FROM AN "AWFUL LITTLE BASEMENT IN A COLD CANADIAN PROVINCE."

I CALL HER "TERRA INFIRMA"—AS A JOKE. BY THE WAY: SHE'S NOT ROMANIAN.

I WONDERED WHAT HER REAL-LIFE COUNTERPART LOOKED LIKE.

Date: Tuesday, 9 February 2006, 9:50 UT
To: Ushio Kawabata <ushio@kyotou.jp>
From: Chickie Levitt <chickie@neuro.usc.edu>
Translation: aml->jpl
Encoding: text:rsa-pubkey

They've done some of that, but still get some distortion. It gets better if the growth is started in the right kind of pre-existing tissue.

I'm thinking of growing a couple of square centimeters of cortical tissue with callosal fibers that seek out and merge with an existing callosum. The DNA hackery would be encoded into an RNA virus deposited on the same electronic chip that contains the digital data interface. The chip would have chemical target sites for one end of the new nerve growth, and would be powered by body metabolism via an integrated ATP fuel cell. Implant the chip somewhere on the edge of the corpus callosum on the brain midline, and the virus will cause the surrounding brain structure to grow a biological data-compressing interface between the chip and the callosum.

The chip must be connected to some kind of external antenna to communicate – maybe a thin wire through the skull, like a hair.

* * * * * * * * * * * * * * * * * * *

Date: Tuesday, 9 February 2006, 9:54 UT
To: Chickie Levitt <chickie@neuro.usc.edu>
From: Ushio Kawabata <ushio@kyotou.jp>
Translation: jpl->aml
Encoding: text:rsa-pubkey

A most interesting proposal! I'll ask Toshi if you can use some of Tskuba's gene-modeling and embryology software to help you with the design. They've become quite good in the last few years.

* * * * * * * * * * * * * * * * * * *

1780 Luigi Galvani demonstrates a connection between nerves, muscles, and electricity by animating frog legs with electricity applied to nerves leading to muscles, thus hinting at how the internal workings of a mind could be coupled to external artificial devices.

1906 Ramon Cajal and Camillo Golgi receive Nobel Prize for developing nerve staining methods, and for elucidating the detailed structure of the cerebrum and cerebelum, thus providing a rough roadmap for later interventions.

1929 Hans Berger invents the electroencephalogram (EEG) for recording electrical activity in the human brain: a crude one-way channel into the functioning of the mind.

1952 James Watson and Francis Crick determine the structure of DNA and its mode of replication, and suggest its role as the control code for biological growth, so laying the foundation for molecular biology, and eventually the engineering of biological structures, including neural assemblies for electronic interfaces.

1953 Wilder Penfield produces maps of the cortex by means of electrical probes of its surface during brain surgery—evoking specific memories, sensations and motor responses by stimulating specific locations, thus establishing the geographic nature of mental organization, and incidentally providing the first example of artificial interaction with the internal workings of the mind.

1959 Robert Noyce and Jack Kirby invent the integrated circuit, a way of placing many electronic components on a single piece of crystal, initiating at least a half-century of exponential growth in electronic complexity, the creation of brain-like machines, and ultimately, artificial minds.

1960 Frank Rosenblatt develops and reports on learning experiments with the Perceptron, an artificial neural net: a way of organizing electronic components in a structure that anatomically and functionally matches the organization of biological brains.

1967 George Brindley and William Lewin implant an electrode array into the visual cortex of a congenitally blind subject, and generate visual phosphenes (spots) by camera-controlled computer activation. This restores some sight to a nerve-blind volunteer, and provides a major early demonstration of computer-nervous system symbiosis.

1969 Dexter Wyckoff and Rajiv Kamar demonstrate the neural comb, a low-noise, high-bandwidth external channel to the nervous system, thus providing, for the first time, potentially total external access to higher mental functions.

1971 Wyckoff, Kamar and Wright use a neural comb with a PDP-10 computer to enable a squirrel monkey to play chess, an early example of mental augmentation by electronic means.

1974 Walter House and Janet Urban install a cochlear implant driven by an external computer, restoring partial hearing to a nerve-deaf patient, and creating a successful medical niche for electronic substitution of lost sensory functions.

1982 William DeVries implants the first permanent artificial heart in a human subject, causing a major shift in the public perception of the relation of "natural" biological functions to "artificial" mechanical devices.

1987 Josephine Bogart and Paul Vogels install a neural comb in the corpus callosum of an epileptic

computer to interrupt seizures: the first human application of a neural comb.

1991 Carver Meade develops an artificial retina, integrating tens of thousands of artificial neurons on an integrated circuit, thus developing some of the analog techniques later used in the electronic portions of "neurochips."

1994 Ushio Kawabata develops a successful predictive model of human cortical behavior based on Edelman's "neural darwinism" formulation, an essential step in providing the engineering environment used to design the neural structures grown by neurochip viruses.

1997 Ushio Kawabata and Chickie Levitt develop an information-efficient method of deriving functional neural anatomy from dense observations of nerve signals, so laying the foundation for the mental mapping process used to adapt a neurochip to its host.

2004 Chickie Levitt and Tosh Okada develop a genetic design for a neural interface between the human callosum and a data transmission integrated circuit. This design is encoded into RNA viruses which are part of neurochip implants, and act by infecting nearby neural tissue, so causing the growth of connective and data compressing neuron structures that connect the electronic portion of the neurochip with the brain.

2006 Chickie Levitt combines previous electronic, genetic and neural innovations to produce a prototype for the first functional self-connecting neurochip.

2007 The first experiment with neurochips is a partial success. A neurochip-augmented chimpanzee demonstrates an equivalent human IQ of 190 for two months before dying of a brain tumor.

Tommy

Total immersion — eighty million polygons per second! He creates worlds and projects them onto the glasses — stereoscopic; you see it in 3-D. The computer senses your movements; makes adjustments as you turn. You're totally inside a synthetic world —

Harry

Too weird! The Web. . . so real! I mean, I've played around with virtual reality toys, but this!

Tommy

Chickie's the icing. The Senator wanted Chickie to work for him. See, Chickie's the Einstein of the New World — the Senator's more like P. T. Barnum. He wants to bring that ballroom in there over the phone lines, right into the living rooms of America. . .

Harry

Whoah. . .

Tommy

That's what 'Church Windows' is all about.

I HEARD TOMMY'S VOICE TELLING ME IT WAS TIME TO GO. BUT I COULDN'T TAKE MY EYES OFF THEM.

THEY BEGAN TO DANCE. I CAN'T TELL YOU HOW EERIE THE WHOLE THING WAS—WHAT BATHOS!

We manufacture our cherished dreams and myths, and project them into all the homes of the world; In one day they create an equality of reality that negates all values. The whole world is a cathedral window, each receiver a soul, our programming the holy message, and wild palms are waved as the saviour sets forth into the holiest of places, riding not an ass but a unicorn back to Coma Berenices.

Now we can record, edit, adjust and transmit our deepest convictions, broadcast in the most mundane parables. In a Synthiotic world, all realities are equal, all actions are equally moral or immoral. Therefore to the New Realist, no action is unacceptable. For we are storming Heaven.

— Anton Kreutzer
On the Way to the Garden

The idea of holography still has an air of magic; this seductive medium of illusionistic three-dimensional space seems the stuff of Disneyland or science-fiction films. Why is the three-dimensional image so fascinating? Over the ages cultures have sought strategies to record the illusion of depth in a two-dimensional plane. For example, the Egyptians flattened and overlapped forms, and artists of the Italian Renaissance invented three-point perspective. This urge to reconcile the visual experience of our world with an image of it has continued into our technological age, from the development of photography to the advanced holography of the Spatial Imaging Group. Positioned at a frontier as photography was a century ago, soon holography will be accessible to the fields of medicine, industrial design, architecture, and beyond, and the potentials of this medium will offer new and visionary images of our world.

The "look" of holography is bound to keep changing as the combination of computers and holography continues to bear fruit beyond our expectations. For most of the world, holography really means "the

psychologically ultimate three-dimensional imaging medium of the future."

...Holograms will inevitably provide moving images, but there has not been much research in holographic movies to date. The Spatial Imaging Group is instead leapfrogging that evolutionary stage, and going directly to the video analog of holography. Broadcasting a conventional hologram would require the spectrum space of 33,000 normal TV channels! Fortunately, most of this information is so over-detailed that much can be left out without human beings even noticing. As computers become bigger and fast enough to efficiently handle the remaining core of information, we have been able to compute and display electronic holographic images in real time for the first time anywhere. We have also developed a new way of showing these images, using an acousto-optical modulator and a spinning mirror system.

To go further, we are developing the new "Ultragram" system mentioned above, which might reach one by three meters in size.

— from *Synthetic Spaces: Holography at MIT*

Television is our new exterior brain. One day it will be a standard fitting within every home on earth, each brain an electronic star in a transmitted Milky Way. Galaxies of dreams and information: people will become more comfortable with televisual reality than with their daily lives. Television will be MORE real than life. A New Reality will dawn, a new synthetic material, giving all people infinite access to infinite alternate realities through a cortex of light. These Realiticians will Program, shape, form, and broadcast our message, until the very fabric of reality has been torn asunder, its cloak cast down beneath the wild palms. From this day forth, reality will be a multiple series of channels, option switches feeding our brains.

— Anton Kreutzer, *Wild Psalms*

THERE WAS SOMETHING GOING ON IN THE BALLROOM OF THE WLSHIRE, AND I DUCKED IN.

NOW TECHNOLOGY FOR CHEAP REALITY IS HERE—AND THE WILD PALMS GROUP IS IN THE EYE OF THE POSTSYMBOLIC STORM. LADIES AND GENTLEMEN, IT IS MY GREAT HONOR, THROUGH THE JOINT EFFORT OF OUR FRIENDS—PARTNERS—IN KAWASAKI AND KANSAI, TO INTRODUCE A VISIONARY: TOMORROW'S REALITICIAN AND TODAY'S BRIDGE BETWEEN HUMAN WETWARE AND HIGH-END TELEPRESENCE...

Senator

I'm not here, children: I am a synthetic hologram, talking to you real-time from the penthouse of this hotel. One day very soon, this is what it's gonna look like, right in the living room — you will co-star in weekly sitcoms; you will fight the samurai battles and experience the heartbreak of first love, all between commercials! If you've got a T.V., any old T.V., and an adaptor you get from Mimecom for under a thousand dollars — then you've bought a ticket. I have seen the future, and it is Channel 3!

As religious plays designed to reveal the mystery of transcendence to men, the earliest theatrical forms were indeed the organization of appearances of their time. And the process of secularization of the theater supplied the models for later, spectacular stage management. Aside from the machinery of war, all machines of ancient times originated in the needs of the theater. The crane, the pulley, and other hydraulic devices started out as theatrical paraphernalia; it was only much later that they revolutionized production relations. It is a striking fact that no matter how far we go back in time the domination of the earth and of men seems to depend on techniques which serve the purposes not only of work but also of illusion.

— Raoul Vaneigem
The Revolution of Everyday Life

CHANGING THE WORLD

WITH PERSONAL REALITY RECORDING

Mimecom's legacy of innovation lives on in the reality tool for a new age!
The result of the most intensive research project in the history of interactive media will soon be in your hands. Developed by Mimecom in conjunction with the realiticians of Kansai and Kawasaki, the new Mimecam2™ lets you make reality recordings as powerful as *ChurchWindows*!
Light, gyro-stabilized, and engineered for durability, with the Mimecam2 and the Mimadaptor,™ you can experience your personal reality recordings in breathtaking Holosynth 3D® — in your own living room!
And the Mimecam2 doesn't just capture the image of the world — it turns your reality into a 3D digital video database that can be manipulated as easily as you captured it! With the Mimedit2™ home editing console, you can clean up that shot of baby's first step. Replay that scene with Dad and design a new ending. Make new memories of old friends. Reality as *you* see it — reality as *you* want it to be. Not since the bit-bare image of Rodney King ignited the first of the L.A. Troubles has a camera had such potential to change the world!
Available soon — wherever fine hometech systems are sold.

Mimecam2™

They Said the Revolution Wouldn't Be Televised.

Senator
 (kisses her)
 Paige Katz!

Paige
 Quite a performance, Senator.

Senator
 Did you really think so?

Paige
 Very Orson Welles — very Mercury
 Theatre.

Senator
 'Invaders From Mars.' We're bringing
 the whole dog and pony show to the
 FCC next week. Think it'll play?

Paige
 If they like Monopoly. Tony, I want
 you to meet a friend of mine — Harry
 Wyckoff.

Paige
 A friend of mine had a dream about
 you. He wants you to come and see
 him, in Rancho Mirage.

Harry
 The Senator?

Paige
 He wanted me to give you this.

She hands him a paper. Harry opens it –
a detailed drawing of a rhino's head.

FADE OUT.

INT. THERAPIST'S
OFFICE — DAY:
Cool, dark office. Harry sits in a
leather chair opposite his
therapist, DR. TOBIAS SCHENKL.

Harry
　　Grace and I haven't made love in two
　　months. That's a record, except for
　　when she had her ectopic.
Tobias
　　It happens. Couples go through
　　periods. . .
Harry
　　You know, I always promised myself
　　a beach house; we were supposed to
　　have a beach house by now. I couldn't
　　even give Grace the money for her
　　store — she had to go to
　　her mother.
Tobias
　　Do you think she loves you any less?
Harry
　　An old lover came to the office this
　　morning; awakened something.
　　(beat)
　　Then, something strange happened, at
　　lunch — sorry I'm so unfocused, Doc.
　　These men came into the restaurant
　　and dragged a guy out; it looked like
　　one of those dumb Robert Longo
　　paintings. Everyone went right back
　　to their meals, like it was all staged
　　or something; like it was nothing.
Tobias
　　You felt. . . vulnerable?
Harry
　　No. I identified with the men.
　　(beat)
　　I was rooting for the attackers.

August 24, 2008

To: United States Senator
Anton Kreutzer
From: Tobias Schenkl, M.D.
Subject: Progress of Therapeutic
Treatment of Harry Wyckoff

　　You have asked me to monitor,
and raise, the emotional temperature of my patient Harry Wyckoff; it
is now quite hot. Within days, it will
reach boiling point. At the same
time, the emotional disequilibrium
will lead to a positive conversion:
the life problems that drove my
patient into treatment will soon
exert an intolerable pressure to find
solutions in the new way of living
that only we and the Church of New
Realism can provide. Both Harry
and his son Coty will soon be ready
for enthusiastic involvement in the
"Church Windows" television program.
　　Harry Wyckoff has been my
patient for four years. During this
time, I have deliberately kept my
therapeutic interventions to an
absolute minimum. In that, to all
appearances, I have merely been
following standard practice — but I
have, in fact, avoided any interpre-
tive hints that would better enable
my patient to put together the
pieces of the puzzle that is his life.
You might say that our relationship
is a holosynth of standard therapeutic treatment: as soon as he
reaches out to touch it, he is grasping at air.
　　During these past four years my
patient has been steadily sliding
into a midlife crisis, the felt reality
of which is in no way diminished by
its banality. Although he has
repeatedly told his wife Grace and
me that Grace is "the best thing
that ever happened to him," he has
never found an adequate object-
substitute to compensate for the
loss of his youthful love, Paige Katz.
To be sure, his marital relationship
is a genuinely loving one — but
although my patient (our patient)
cannot admit this to himself, he is
subliminally aware that he is unful-
filled. And now that we have engineered the reappearance of Ms.
Katz, that awareness is about to
erupt.
　　The fundamental ground of my
patient's dissatisfaction, however,
lies in the insecurity attendant
upon not having known his parents.
Never having met his father, who
died a few years after he was born,
and having no memory of his men-
tally disturbed mother, from whom
he was parted soon after, my
patient is lacking in those intro-
jected sources of parental affection
so essential to self-esteem, and for
which his adult life has provided no
workable substitutes. Knowing

I WENT AND SAW MY OLD SHRINK. HE SAID I WAS ADDICTED TO TURMOIL.

YOU TURN EVERYTHING INTO SHIT.

SOMETIMES HE'S COLD, TO MAKE A POINT. STILL, HE SCARES ME.

this, I have taken care not to give him anything more than a simulation of support, in order to drive the sense of loss and emptiness to ever-higher levels. Hence, my patient is both homeless and directionless, and he will remain so until you and Channel 3 take him in.

In fact, he is even homeless at home, because of his increasing inability to play the role of father to his son. Though he is devoted to his two children, his and his wife's relationship with their son has become disturbed. Like the school counselors, Harry and his wife ascribe their son's growing coldness and violent outbreak at school today to Coty's being at a "difficult age." That is true, so far as it goes — but what is really happening is that he is catching glimpses, in his dreams, of the alternate reality for which he has always longed. Actually, my patient, too, is at a "difficult age" — and glimpsing another world. The dreams that he and his son have begun to share are driving them both toward the virtual reality of Channel 3, which offers sources of satisfaction not to be found within the family walls. But Harry's visions torment him; his son Coty welcomes them.

The lack of satisfaction in his family relationships is directly paralleled by the frustration of his professional life. Although my patient is a successful and respected lawyer, the emotional situation here is the same as that prevailing with his wife: a substitute gratification that is satisfying so far as it goes but that does not offer compensations equal to those of what is missed. Put otherwise, my patient can find no meaning in his job.

Even at a more mundane level of satisfaction — financial satisfaction — my patient feels a gap, a lack. He is about to make partner in his firm; however, he has not yet achieved the income at which he had been aiming, and he feels guilty for not having been able to lend financial support to his wife's business or buy himself and his family the beach house that he had sworn would be theirs at this point. I asked him yesterday whether he really felt that his wife loved him any the less, and this particular question was sincerely compassionate — but I knew that it would do him little good. It is clear to me that if a man like my patient, lacking a sense of accomplishment in his life as a whole, feels unable to meet even his more modest expectations, he will be all the more oppressed by the sense of his own incapacity.

I was, then, in no way surprised to learn from my patient that he has been sexually dysfunctional for two months. He feels himself to be impotent, and so he is.

With this sense of both spiritual and bodily impotence has come the desire to lash out. My patient is conscious of violent, as yet undirected, urges. He told me yesterday that a few hours earlier, when he had witnessed a mysterious attack and abduction in a chic restaurant (apparently carried out by agents of the Wild Palms Group, to judge by his description), he felt not pity or fear but a desire to join in. The desire for violence — to "hit back" — is thus nicely advanced, and it will require only further hints from me and another approach from you (say, an invitation to Wild Palms) to

be channelled in the socially positive direction we have set for the country.

The surfacing of violent urges has been facilitated by those magnificently vivid dreams to which he has been subject and which I have encouraged him to regard as what they are: evidences of a breakthrough. Above all, the repeated encounter in his house with a rhinoceros reveals to him, and will further provoke in him, a not-so-latent desire to enter the world of bestial savagery—which is, after all, not so far from the world in which we are already living. And the tattoo of wild palms that he saw on his wife's body in last night's vision corresponds to his desire for himself and his family to be imprinted with such a world, to carry it with them.

Harry Wyckoff is a man with an enormous capacity for love — and with it, an enormous ambition — that has not yet found its proper objects. When the proper objects of personal and professional fulfillment are held out to him, as they already have begun to be — through yourself, his new job at Channel 3, and Paige Katz — he will leap to embrace them.

Granted: his needs may never be satisfied by reality, especially the needs deriving from his childhood; perhaps those desires could have been satisfied only in a world that is long-since drowned. But we offer him a substitute reality that is better than the real article — an artificial limb more mobile than a leg. With light rays and electrical waves, we give back everything that was lost.

We fuck with the mind from love.

INT. WYCKOFF HOUSE —
LIVING/DINING ROOM — DAY:
Grace and Coty enter. Coty plunks
himself in front of TV. Harry, in
apron, enters from Kitchen with
Deirdre in arms.

Grace
    (to Coty) Tell Daddy what happened.
    Come on, tell him.
    (Coty ignores her.)
Grace
    Mister Cool Customer.
Harry
    Kill someone at school?
Grace
    Coty. . .
Coty
    I'm gonna be on television.
Grace
    Tabba's new show, 'Church
    Windows.'
Harry
    How'd that happen?
Grace
    We had lunch. She said they were
    looking for a twelve-year-old kid for
    her show. I told her about Coty and
    she said, bring him in.
Coty
    (re: TV show) Quiet!

When official science has come
to such a pass, like all the rest of
the social spectacle that for all its
materially modernized and
enhanced presentation is merely
reviving the ancient techniques
of fairground mountebanks —
*illusionists, barkers, and stool-
pigeons* — it is not surprising to
see a similar and widespread
revival of the authority of seers
and sects, of vacuum-packed Zen
or Mormon theology. Ignorance,
which has always served the
authorities well, has also always
been exploited by ingenious
ventures on the fringes of the
law. And what better moment
than one where illiteracy has
become so widespread? But this
reality in its turn is denied by a
new display of sorcery....

— Guy Debord
*Comments on the Society
of the Spectacle*

Suddenly, a group of actors is dropped down into the Wyckoff living room: the HOLOSYNTH Coty, Tabba — and a REALTOR, who's "showing" them their new home. Deirdre goes over to Coty's HOLOSYNTH, mesmerized by the HOLO–SYNTHS. Coty darts about, playfully "shadowing" his HOLOSYNTH, mimicking dialog and movements; Harry has to restrain him.

Tabba
   (looks around room)
   Hmmm. Not bad. Needs a little
   fixing up. . .
Coty
   (protesting) But, Ma —
Realtor
   We handle all kinds of unusual
   properties. Moved a young couple
   into an old mortuary last week —
   very chic.
Coty
   To die for.

LAUGHTRACK.

Realtor
   When did you say you lost your
   husband?
Coty
   (sotto; contemptuous) Nice segue.

LAUGHTRACK.

Tabba
   A year ago. The strange thing is, he
   was a minister. . .

INT. WILD PALMS — NIGHT:
Paige and the Senator are watching.

Realtor
   Then it's perfect. And the price
   is right. It's close to the schools —
   and to God: He's a local call.
Tabba
   Not everyone can say they have
   the Almighty as a landlord.
Coty
   Emphasis on **Lord**.

Win a DREAM DATE with COTy!

Hi all you rabid fans of Coty Wyckoff, 12, the hot new hunk of Channel 3's biggest hit ever! Of course we're talking about the large, the ultra (it's frighteningly huge, huh?) series "Church Windows." Well, you will be happy to know that Coty's just a regular almost-teenage guy! To prove it, he recently invited **TEENDREAMS** to visit him at home, where he lives with his parents (still together!) and his sweet little sister Deirdre. We sat in the cozy den, surrounded by his personal possessions — comic books, a pair of Nike Ultra-Elite 2000s, a framed photo of his Uncle Tony and a copy of the same uncle's book; *Confessions of A Go Master*. Then the mega-talented heartthrob revealed to us such supercharged morsels as his starsign (he's a steamy Scorpio, of course), his fave color ("dark black") and what he wants in a girl. So read on DREAMers, and don't forget to fill out the ballot below — cause we'll be sending one of you (plus a lucky chaperone) on an intimate night on the town with Coty and his grandma (you know her as Josie Ito)! Enter now and *dream on*.

TEENDREAMS: *Let's start right off with the first questions on all our readers' lips. What kind of girl really turns you on, and is there a special female in your life?*

COTY: Well, my sister, Deirdre, is truly wonderful. I certainly wish more women could be like her. As is Josie, my grandmother, whom you know has been much more than a relative to me — she has helped me tremendously with my career. I will always love her for that. Josie has also shown me that I am not like everyone else. She has instilled in me a special sense of purpose based on that knowledge. She explains my dreams.

TD: *Ooh, now we're talking! What are your dreams about, Coty?*

C: Animals and things. Normal stuff.

TD: *And what kind of music are you into?*

C: I like old stuff. Psychic TV. And I love Wagner.

TD: *We notice you talk a lot about your grandmother, and you're always discussing your uncle and his work, and we know about your on-screen mom, but you haven't mentioned your off-screen parents. Can you tell us about them?*

C: No comment. No, really, it's just that I don't feel it's fair to bring press attention to people who have not chosen to put themselves in the spotlight, under public scrutiny, as I have. So that's why I don't discuss them. *(Readers: He's sensitive, too! Swoon!)*

TD: *"Church Windows" is a major mega hit. When did you know you were involved with something so super special?*

C: I knew we had a hit on our hands after our first week on the air, when I was at the mall with Josie and got mobbed by fans. The people were so very warm, so loving, so friendly.

TD: *Now for a toughie: Do you ever find, now that you are such a huge star, that other kids are intimidated by you, or jealous of all your success?*

C: There is no me they could be jealous of. Everyone has their own idea of me. Everyone owns me. I mean, I visit my fans every day in their living rooms, so we are very close. It's way too intimate for intimidation. Besides, I have a sense of higher purpose with all this that I'd like to pass on to other kids too, and that comes from learning about my uncle's New Realism, which I'd be happy to explain in more detail if anyone wants to contact me through the Coty Fan Club.

(Note to readers: Isn't he smart, girls? Just like his character, Ivan!)

TD: *Good answer. A lot of your fans out there would probably love to follow in your footsteps and become actors too. Can you tell them, is being a big TV star all it's cracked up to be?*

C: It's the best thing to happen since the dawn of time. And with the technology we have now, with Mimecams, anybody can find out exactly what it's like to be not only an actor but a big star themselves. Everyone should try it.

TD: *What's next for you?*

C: I've been approached about a new series called "What's Not To Love?," and I've also gotten a lot of movie interest, so you may see me on the big screen before long. And then, who knows where I might go from there? As I've said, I have larger interests outside the whole acting arena.

TD: *Well, Coty, we think we speak for ourselves and all the **TEENDREAMS** readers around the world when we say we'll follow you anywhere!*

In the meantime guys, for those dull hours when "Church Windows" isn't on, check out the dreamy life-size Coty pull-out poster on page 29. It's 3-D, of course, and perfect for a sorority-house door or bedroom ceiling. And keep dreaming — cause you never know when they might come true!

EVERYTHING WENT RATHER WELL, EXCEPT FOR THE LAST WEEK OF SHOOTING, WHEN A CRAZY MAN BURST ONTO THE SET.

I'M BUD WIGGINS, DAMMIT! I HAVE CHRONIC SINUSITIS! THEY DIDN'T REVIEW ME IN THE VLS! SOMEONE GET ME WOLF SOLENT AND BURGESS'S RE JOYCE! SCHWARTZKOF AND HER FUCKING FATHERS HAVE DESTROYED ME!

2 KCBS PENDLETON GROVE — Drama: 60 min. (cc)
A rash of brutal animal sacrifices draws suspicion on young Lysander (Kyle Delacroix); Mrs. Sturtevant (Justine Bateman) suffers a mild stroke at a virtual reality theme park, causing the reclusive monk Shoki (George Takai) to leave his Ashram and become her principal care-giver.

4 KNBC CUT AND RUN — Sitcom: 30 min. (cc)
A mysterious stranger comes to town and maliciously degausses everybody's digital media; Falasha (Taneesha Omar) tries to lure Ryan away from his Twelve Step program with spicy Cajun home cookin' and the promise of unprotected sex; Matty develops an odd obsession with "ethnic cleansing."

5 KTLA MOVIE — Drama: 2 hrs. ★★
"CANCER CLUSTER" (2002) Macaulay Culkin stars as a crusading muckraker who, in spite of his own terminal leukemia, takes on the powerful petrochemical interests he suspects of poisoning his entire town. Griffin O'Neill, Marky Mark and Lisa Bonet also star.

7 KABC 21ST CENTURY SCHIZOID MAN — Cyber Adventure: 60 min. (cc)
Branca (Eusebio Choi) accidentally ingests micron-sized Japanese medical robots that have been programmed to kill by the grasping, evil Dr. Telluride (Mandy Patinkin).

9 KCAL BLASKO'S WORLD — Sitcom: 30 min. (cc) (Repeat)
A genetic engineer has Blasko (Tom Selleck) doubting the viability of his gametes following a mishap with a high energy microwave dish; Candace (Su-zanne Dimitri) tells Bobby (Vinny Krakow) that the guy he's dating isn't a guy at all but a deliciously hunky "trans."

11 FOX/MURDOCH ONE WARNING! SEX OFFENDER! THE ATASCADERO FILES — Reality: 60 min. (cc)

Scheduled: A convicted child molester attempts suicide with an overdose of Prozac; Veteran guard gives guided tour of the maximum security "Perv Pit"; Elderly inmate looks forward to early release only to be re-arrested for fondling Parole Officer.

11 A FOX/MURDOCH TWO DUC CASH FLOW SYSTEM — Paid Infomercial: 2 hrs.
Real Estate whiz Nguyen Cao Duc explains how to "turn the misfortune of others into good fortune for you"; Host: James Spader.

11 B FOX/MURDOCH THREE 90210 2000 — Drama: 60 min. (cc)
Brenda (Shannon Doherty) resigns her Republican Senate Seat to donate a kidney for transplantation into deathly ill brother Brandon (Jason Priestly); Dylan (Luke Perry) faces indictment following whispered allegations of wrongdoing at the pre-school.

13 KCOP THE JULIA ROBERTS SHOW — Interview: 30 min.
Scheduled Topics: "Women Who Masturbate"; Controversial artist Tully Woiwode defends his recent exhibition of retouched, defaced David Hockneys.

28 KCET "FRONTLINE" — Investigative: 90 min. (cc)
"SEALED WITH A FLAW" — Did utilities lobbyist and former Vice President Dan Quayle knowingly obstruct the Atomic Energy Commission's investigation of last year's catastrophic meltdown of Indiana Light and Power's Reactor Number Nine? Host: Judy Woodruff.

36 THE I.A.N. NETWORK — Armenian Specialty Programming.

WILD PALMS ONE (2-D) CROSS CURRENTS — Public Affairs: 60 min. (cc)
Topic: "Is All This Beastliness Strictly Necessary?" Scheduled Guest: Josie Kreutzer-Ito, Director of Senator Anton "Tony" Kreutzer's campaign, discusses the media's role in recent allegations of fraud, mind-control and sexual impropriety hurled against the Senator in his current reelection drive. Host: Peter Jennings.

WILD PALMS TWO (3-D Holographic Interactive) (Decoder Required) CHURCH WINDOWS — Sitcom: 30 min.
Young Ivan (Coty Wyckoff) gets in hot water at school for making precocious comments to his Principal, Mrs. Scanlon (Ellen Barkin); Rushing to prepare for her "hot date" with a divorced doctor (Neil Patrick Harris) Tabba (Tabba Schwartzkopf) confuses flea dip for home perm with hilarious results.

A&E DOCUMENTARY — 2 hrs. 30 min. ★★★★ — (cc) (Repeat)
"THE CALIES: HARD ROAD TO NOWHERE" — Distinguished journalist Maury Povich's hard-hitting portrait of the modern day "Dust Bowl" reverse-migration of Californians desperately taking to the roads in search of a better life in the East. Povich's camera crew follows a broken former Disney executive as he piles his family and his few remaining possessions into a battered BMW and hits the road in a pathetic quest for hope.

HBO THE LANNIE GREENBERGER SHOW — Interview: 30 min.
Paroled "Cotton Club Murder" conspirator explores subjects of current interest. Scheduled topic: "Are Your Thighs All They Could Be?"

NIPPON NETWORK "ASAHI — THE SUN RISES FOR US" — Pacific Rim Current Events: 60 min. (cc)
Host Noriko Sora interviews disgraced former Supreme Court Justice Clarence Thomas; Luxury golfing in the Andes; "Hello Kitty" turns 30; A holographic home tour of Graceland!

SHOW MOVIE — Action Comedy: 2 hrs. ★
"ROAD KILL" (2003) — A neurotic Manitoba grandmother (Goldie Hawn), fearing the onset of Alzheimer's, O.D.s on Vasopressin and embarks on a hell-bent demolition derby rampage across the Canadian tundra. Lou Diamond Phillips, Anna Chlumsky and Garth Brooks also star.

TBS MOVIE — Musical: 2 1/2 hrs. ★
"SHARP!" (1996) Gary Coleman and Louis Gossett Jr. star in Spike Lee's troubled screen adaptation of the Andrew Lloyd Webber Broadway musical depicting the rise and fall of urban demagogue Al Sharpton.

MTV "MICHAEL, MICHAEL, WHEREFORE ART THOU, MICHAEL?" — Music, Variety: 4 hrs. (Repeat)
Gala Memorial Concert for the late Michael Jackson held at England's Wembley Stadium with appearances by Quincy Jones, Diana Ross, Barbra Streisand, The Berlin Philharmonic, and the "Over The Hill All-Star Review" featuring Axl Rose, Madonna, Sinead O'Connor, Paul McCartney, Bruce Springsteen and Ice-T. Host: Macaulay Culkin.

WGN MOVIE — Melodrama: 3 1/2 hrs. ★★
"RICKSHAW MAN" (2005) In Oliver Stone's screen adaptation of Jay McInerny's best-seller, Tabba Schwartzkopf stars as a self-loathing sexaholic pop star who, following a near-fatal plane crash, finds hope, love and redemption through an unlikely liason with a blind Okinawan street beggar (Haruomi Hosono). Liam Neeson, Rie Miyazawa and Brad Dourif also star.

I SPOKE TO HIM BEFORE THE POLICE ARRIVED. HE SAID HE WAS FROM BANNING. HE WAS POIGNANTLY LUCID AND KEPT APOLOGIZING HIS 'DIALOGUE' WASN'T 'LINEAR' ENOUGH. HE PLEADED THAT IN THE FUTURE, HIS 'STORYLINE' WOULD BE 'LESS LIKE A DREAM,' EASIER TO FOLLOW. STRANGE, MOVING FELLOW.

How would you like to work for me?

Harry

Doing what?

Senator

(caddy places ball on tee)
We'd have to find something. Household chores, maybe?
Can always use another masseur. How about head of
business affairs at Channel 3, at five times your old salary?
(He tees off.)

Harry

(dodges dirt clump)
Are you kidding?

Senator

Absolutely not.

Harry

Why me?

Senator

Two reasons: because I dreamt about Harry Wyckoff and
the unicorn — and because when you were just a boy, you
ran away. . . to the desert.

Jorge Luis Borges, in his *Book of Imaginary Beings*, had
this to report on the Chinese variant of the legendary
beast called *k'i-lin*:

"When Confucius' mother bore him in her womb,
the spirits of the five planets brought her an animal
'having the shape of a cow, the scales of a dragon, and
a horn on its forehead.' This is the way Soothill reports
the annunciation: a variant of this given by Wilhelm
tells that the animal appeared on its own and spat out
a jade tablet on which these words were read:
    Son of mountain crystal [or the essence of water],
when the dynasty crumbles, thou shalt rule as a
throneless king.
    Seventy years later, some hunters killed a *k'i-lin*
which still had a bit of ribbon around its horn that
Confucius' mother had tied there. Confucius went to
look at the Unicorn and wept because he felt what the
death of this innocent and mysterious animal foretold,
and because in that ribbon lay his past."

Alain Bosquet: If you were not a human being, what animal would you like to be?

Salvador Dali: Always the same, a rhinoceros, because the rhinoceros is the only animal that carries an incredible sum of cosmic knowledge inside its armor.

Coty
    It's a wise father that knows his own child.
    (whispers in Harry's ear)
    There are so many enemies on the way to the garden. . .

Woiwode
    Still having the visions, Harry?
Gavin
    The rhino's key, Harry. We all saw the rhino.
Stitch
    Not everyone sees the rhino.
Gavin
    I would kill for some onion soup.
Woiwode
    Lose your self-importance: no one cares about Harry Wyckoff. You think the Senator cares?
Harry
    Look: I'm not interested in anything political. Let me go, Gavin. I have a family. . .
Gavin
    You mean a semblance of a family —

89

INT. WYCKOFF HOUSE —
LIVING ROOM — DAY:
Grace sits on the floor in the
darkened room. She's been drinking;
spread out before her is a massive
jigsaw puzzle.

<u>Grace</u>
How was it?

<u>Harry</u>
Pretty amazing. He's got a house
the size of a country club.

<u>Grace</u>
(ironic) Are you a spokesman for
Synthiotics now?

<u>Harry</u>
Not quite. But he asked me to work
for him.

<u>Grace</u>
(stands; goes to wetbar)
Gonna do it?

<u>Harry</u>
It's a lot of money. I just have to
figure out what I'm getting myself
into.

<u>Grace</u>
Drink?
(after a beat)
Why didn't you tell me about her?

Dearest Father,

Each time I begin a letter to you, I'm overwhelmed by —
what is this feeling? Is it love? Terror? I pray that it isn't
hatred. I don't want to be like Josie.

She loved you. Was it frightening? Was she too hungry? When you left her, she died of starvation. That's
what Josie is now, Father: a hungry ghost.

I'm pregnant again. I've got that vintage sci-fi horror
show feeling deep down inside: "*My God, Captain! It's-
it's alive!*" But I am not with child. No, this time around
I have a belly full of secrets. Talk about heartburn! Harry
tries so hard to help me, to make me comfortable, to be
understanding. He puts pillows under my feet, he
brings me soda crackers, he strokes my hair through
tearful fits of hysteria. And I just smile at him, a miserable sphinx.

No wonder Harry turns away. Adultery is such a hopeful pose. I like it in him. I do! When Harry and I were in
the thick of passion I could never quite believe it. At
least now I can see that it was true. True love! There
aren't even words for all of my secrets. My God, the poor
man! It's hard being an innocent bystander (don't I know

Harry

Paige? I don't know — it was all a long time ago. Maybe I should have.

Grace

Were you still seeing her? When we first met?

(beat)

Don't lie to me, Harry.

Harry

No. It was over, a few months before.

Grace

Is it over now?

Harry

Yes.

Grace

Got you on the rebound, huh.

Harry

You're the best thing that ever happened to me, Grace.

Grace

I used to think so.

(stands)

I have a headache. I'm gonna take a nap.

Harry

I love you.

Grace

(reaches stairs; without looking back)

Love you, too. It's a world filled with giant love-bugs.

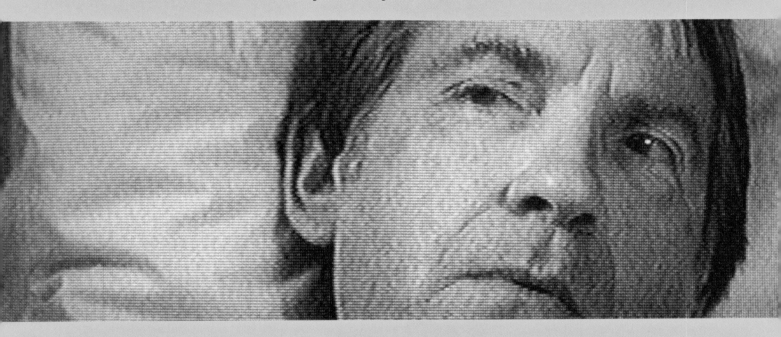

it). Oh, the insidious treachery of women! Poor Harry.

A happy marriage. Isn't that what Josie wanted with you? If Harry leaves me, what will I become? Another mortally wounded monster? I should kill myself now before it's too late. It may be the only way to save Harry and the children. Was that my ambition all along — to be the first woman on earth to die peacefully of a happy marriage? Lay the ghosts to rest?

Every day at about four-thirty I stop whatever I'm doing and think about suicide. No romantic brooding, just a minor decision, to be or not to be, a normal part of a normal day in the life of Grace Wyckoff. This is how I fool myself into thinking I have self-control. In fact, I have none. I am weak.

So what do you think, father, should I kill myself today?

A fitting epiphany for the daughter of a "great man." What an unfunny joke that would be! The martyred housewife. Can't you just see me in my Armani bathrobe and slippers, tacked up on the cross? Hilarious, if you ask me. "Our Fathers, who art dead and in prison, hollow be thy names. . ."

I'm not afraid of ghosts. Hell, Eli, I'm the daughter of

ghosts. Yesterday, Coty asked me where my daddy was. I told him my daddy was dead. He called me a liar. I don't know what Josie has been telling him. But Coty's right. I am a liar. I lie to Harry, I lie to Coty, I lie to myself.

The way you lied to me — subtly, despite years of corrosive silence. Can you ever forgive me for your lies? I don't care about lies. There are no lies in the floating world, only illusions. I'm getting seasick, Goddamn it! Just kidding. The eskimos have 349 words for snow. The Japanese have over a thousand words for bullshit, each one more beautiful than the next. . .

I want to plant myself on your doorstep and say, "Love me, daddy, please!" But I can't. I'm too afraid of what will happen to me. Damn it! If you had loved Josie enough none of this would be happening. Is it your fault? Could I have loved her enough in your stead? She's the only person who really knows me. If I died today she would be my soul's executor. But Friends are evil, treacherous, aren't they? That's what Josie taught me.

The words burn to get out, but they settle lightly on the tear-soaked page like ashes floating on still, deep water. Oh yes, I'll say anything for effect. That's all it is, of course. My lies. . .

[Partial transcript of a television interview with convicted attempted assassin Sonya Lynn Lefebre. Interview conducted and broadcast October 30, 2007 on "The Jerry Rivers Show."]

J R : *As Tony Kreutzer left the Century Plaza hotel following a Rebuild LA reunion, you were cold-bloodedly waiting for him with a curare-tipped blow dart —*

S L : Yeah, damn straight. Hey, World War III is being fought RIGHT NOW by self-proclaimed "techno-shamans" against all free human and wildlife on this planet. Mimecom is a multi-dimensional corporate death machine! We are up against an undeclared menticide more dangerous than any genocide waged thus far. These are the last days — planetarily-speaking. This is worldwide perceptual holy war!

Look, Anton Kreutzer is already vastly more powerful than any other elected official in this country. President Colin Powell is just Howdy-Doody — get it— the ultimate ass-licking Student Body President.

J R : *You have been diagnosed as paranoid schizophrenic. Your motives have been described by leading forensic psychiatrists as "delusional fantasies". Why should we believe that one of America's most successful entrepeneurs, a true folk-hero, is actually a blood-thirsty cult leader?*

S L : What I think your viewers need to understand is that New Realism represents the total crystallization of a dying order — you may not see it, but the spectacle is already fragmenting. . . When I took up my blowgun against Anton Kreutzer, it was the first time in my life I actually felt alive. You know, much more blood will have to be shed to wrest control of the means of perception back to the people. We, the Friends, must slice through the power of illusion with the diamond-hard purity of our vision.

The funny thing is. . . when Eli Levitt was sent away to rot in the Perceptory gulag, it was already too late. There's too many of us now. His word is spreading like an incurable virus. We will tear apart what remains of this worthless rag that you call a social fabric.

J R : *Sonya, let's face it: you didn't exactly start out as a Lee Harvey Oswald or Arthur Bremer type. You seem to be an intelligent woman, even if you are completely bonkers. How the heck did you get this chip on your shoulder about Synthiotics?*

S L : Jerry, I don't believe that condescending tone is warranted on your part. When I first arrived in Brazil as a young Maryknoll Missionary Sister, I guess I was all set to be the next Mother Teresa. . . I subsequently left my Order when I began to realize that the Faith I had been raised in was actually a twisted, patriarchal conspiracy against the simple believers of this Earth.

You know it's funny, when I was a Sister, they were always warning us against having "particular friendships" inside the convent. Not that it stopped us, of course. But now I have Friends who I am spiritually linked to in the struggle for true vision all over the globe. . .

J R : *Wait a sec, let's get back on track here — why Tony Kreutzer of all people?*

S L : Seeing the Earth, Gaia, our mother, gouged out and violated like I did in Minais Gerais, made me want to get involved with the dedicated people who were organizing to protect the Amazon rain forest. Since I was already fluent in Portuguese, I got a staff position with the Rain Forest Defense Fund. It didn't take me long to realize there was something fishy going on there. RFDF is a front for a whole range of covert Synthiotics activities in Latin America. . .

J R : *Wow, that's heavy. So you're saying that this organization isn't really about "save the trees" and that you decided to investigate the Synthiotics organization on your own?*

S L : It has been thoroughly documented that they [Synthiotics operatives] contracted with the Brazilian municipal governments to obtain [makes "air quotes" with two fingers of each hand] unwanted children to test their mind control drugs on. There was a seemingly endless supply of young human guinea pigs, these poor abandoned orphans from the favelas, for their Pharms. One of the American doctors I met at a secret Amazon compound, said he had been kicked out of UCLA's NPI for hot-rodding his electro-shock unit without proper authorization back in the '80's. As soon as the Fathers heard he was finally cited by the NIMH review board, they had him flying down to Rio on the next Varig plane out of LAX.

J R : *It definitely sounds like a pretty wild scene down there, Sonya. Now who put you up to trying to take out Tony Kreutzer? If you can tell us anything without endangering yourself?*

S L : Let's just say we have some "friends in high

places," actually moles in the State Department's Latin American section, gave me the orders to get in touch with certain high-level Columbian "import-export" execs. Then, I was met by a contact who I knew only as "Hector" at the Medellin airport. I was immediately given two months of intensive training in disguise, currency manipulation, remote communications, and of course, short-range assassination, by what I would call some real experts.

J R : *Why would the Medellin cartel, some pretty hard-headed guys I would think, want to help you in your loony celebrity-stalking?*

S L : Simple. They wanted to whack Kreutzer. His "interactive" synthetic street compounds was gaining way too much market share on rock cocaine. At least crackheads are conversational. To me there's nothing scarier than this new generation of video-fiend "supermarios" that Kreutzer is creating. The Japanese slang word for them is "otaku." I mean there have been cases of twelve-year old kids dead of autoerotic asphyxia after watching re-runs of Jessica Hahn's 976 ads while high on street interactives — it's so *sad*. I mean it's all too real for them.

Anyway, so Herr Kreutzer is way too connected in the Beltway for them to do anything about this unprecedented competition without maintaining "plausible deniability." The enemy of my enemy — they knew that the Friends aren't afraid to die. Hey, all of us have to die sometime. Even high-tech media moguls.

J R : *Sonya, I'm still asking you one simple question: Why did you do it?*

S L : Kreutzer's true thought, the hermetic meaning of Synthiotics, represents an all-out war against the life-force itself. He is the penultimate Man of Negation. Just read his books! The whole plan is already laid out! Kreutzer wants to bring on a worldwide Jonestown and nothing less. If you've seen the sad, scrambled face of a "smart-memory"-ravaged Brazilian child like I have, then you can't just kick back and watch Channel 3 anymore.

J R : *Now, you have already made some rather bizarre allegations about certain rock personalities being in on what you call the Big Con —*

S L : As part of the Rain Forest Defense Fund, I personally saw Sting, the rock singer, embrace local Synthiotics functionaries and accept an honorary rhino necklace at one of our conclaves. At the time, he told me he was into "collecting endangered species stuff."

J R : *Are you saying that Sting has been hoodwinked by a nefarious bunch of computer nerds?*

S L : I'm just saying: Look at his new album, *Unicorn Tails*, it says right on the back cover, "Spiritual Advisor: Anton Kreutzer". What about songs like "Shape-Shifter," "Dimensional Portals" —

J R : *OK, OK, enough tea-leaf reading, Sonya — now one of the Mimecom security personnel, Kurt Spaeter, is lying on the brink of death in the twilight world of a poison-induced coma. I think what we all would really like to know is, are you truly sorry for what you did?*

S L : Definitely! Sorry the bastard isn't dead yet. . . The time is coming soon when we will give Mr. Kreutzer his exit visa and alter his reality in a very permanent way [laughs].

J R : *Alright, now we know you hate the Pope, you think Synthiotics is a cult, the U.S. government is a sham, but what do you believe in, Sonya?*

S L : The Earth, the Sky, the Moon — what I can see. The real question is [gestures pointedly with both hands, faces camera directly]: are you down with the worldwide anti-spectacular urban guerilla struggle?

J R : *Can you translate that last part into English for me and the viewers?*

S L : OK, reality-check, big-time! Let me break it down for you—

In this society, the highest degree of illusion has come to have the highest degree of sacredness. Until the sick lie of "freedom of information" is exposed for what it is, the only option that remains for us is the Propaganda of the Deed [points at Rivers]. That's the only reason I agreed to let a sexist, pandering, hypocritical piece of shit like you interview me in the first place.

We are engaging in active resistance against the hidden repression of despotic reality engineers. The Friends are creating Revolutionary media sabotage through the autonomous actions of self-liberated individuals. If the mediaplex wants a "mad dog," it will create one for its own vicarious thrills. Personally, I just didn't like what I was seeing and decided to do something about it.

J R : *We understand from one of your former cellmates that you had a secret hit list that extended to other prominent Americans far beyond just Tony Kreutzer. Can you tell us who was next on your sick list?*

S L : Yeah, sure, what the hell. . . Camille Paglia.

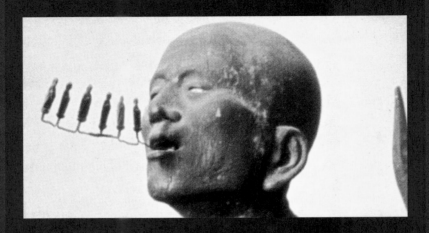

INT. PERCEPTORY — VISITING
ROOM — DAY:
Grace and her father continue their
dialogue; she looks drawn and
fragile — emotional — leading up to
something.

Grace
I know that the Fathers have done
terrible things. I know that they have
taken children from political enemies;
that they have harvested children.
What I need to know, is . . . my son
Coty. . . Is it possible — I know they
consider me one of their own — they
would have to —

Eli
What is it, Grace?
Grace
Would they have taken Coty and
given me the son of another? Could
they have done that? Answer me,
Father!

The eradication of the tyrannical nuclear family: building-block of the prison walls for this imposed humanitarian dust, that chokes and dulls the masses, reducing all to a worthless, mindless, dreamless fog.

We perpetuate our tyranny and drown in a flood of speculation and false communication. To be reborn, immortal, outside Time, we must look for ways to transmit multiple realities and to make them as real, MORE real than the emasculating reductions that we inherit; corrupted and trivialized by a belief in their singularity. Nothing is real, everything must go.

Every inherited construct, society, or techno-patriotic political system must be destroyed as fast as possible. We must MAKE SPACE TO BE SPACE. This is the New Realist position.

— Anton Kreutzer, *Wild Psalms*

CABANA:

Once out of guests' sight, she viciously punches Grace in the gut. Grace doubles over, reeling into wall.
Then she gut-punches her again.

<u>Josie</u>

You've got a hell of a mouth on you: watch someone doesn't take a needle and sew it up.

<u>Grace</u>

You leave that little boy alone!

<u>Josie</u>

Don't insult me by pretending you don't know what's happening! You knew from the beginning — **weak dog!** Listen to me: we
have come too far to be terrorized by your prim sensitivities — do I make myself clear?
(slaps her again)
Answer me!

<u>Grace</u>

Yes!

MY LIFE WAS FILLED WITH BROKEN CHILDREN.
WHO WAS THIS GIRL BUT ANOTHER RUINED
NURSERY RHYME?

THE GIRL WAS ME.

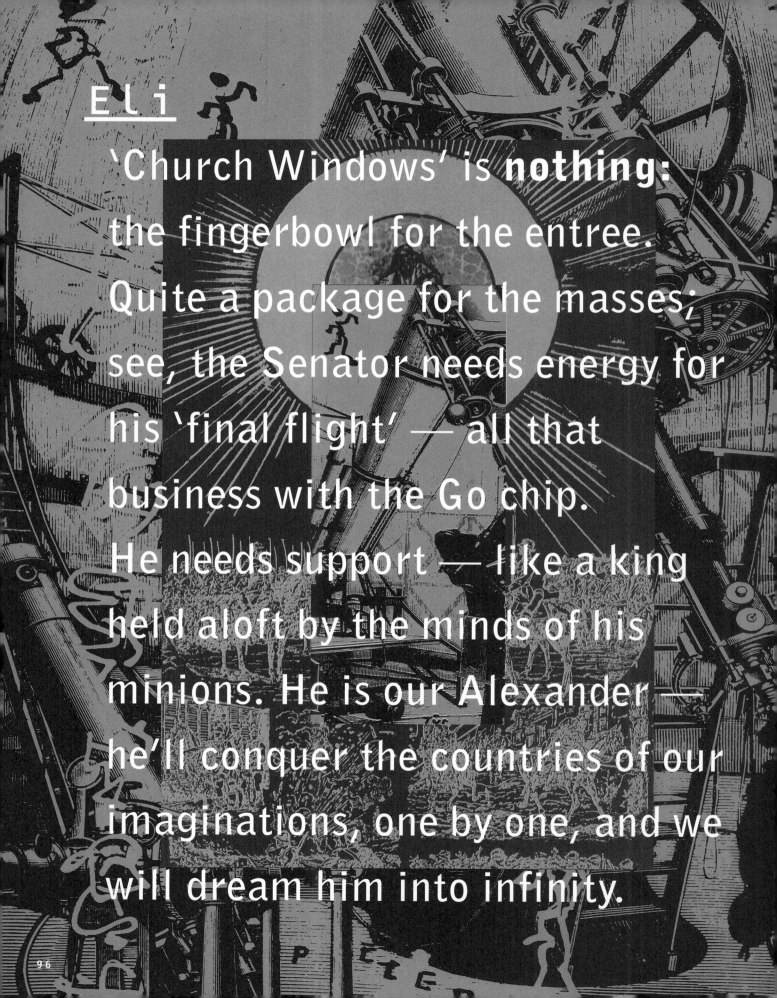

ELi

'Church Windows' is **nothing:** the fingerbowl for the entree. Quite a package for the masses; see, the Senator needs energy for his 'final flight' — all that business with the Go chip. He needs support — like a king held aloft by the minds of his minions. He is our Alexander — he'll conquer the countries of our imaginations, one by one, and we will dream him into infinity.

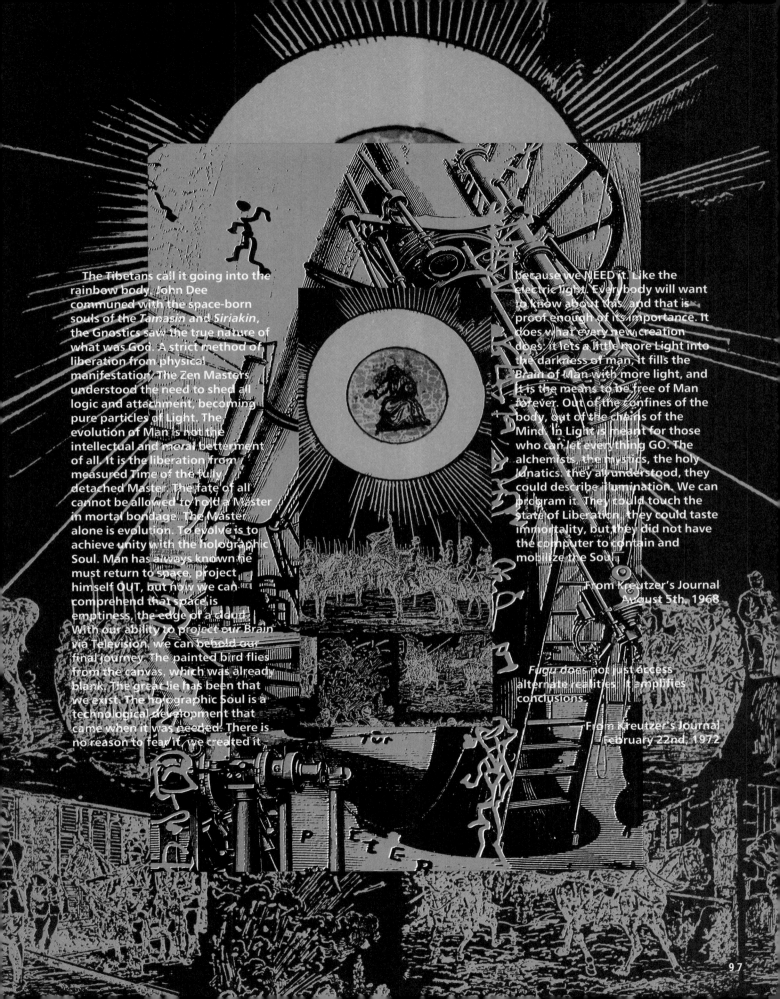

The Tibetans call it going into the rainbow body. John Dee communed with the space-born souls of the *Tamasin* and *Siriakin*, the Gnostics saw the true nature of what was God. A strict method of liberation from physical manifestation. The Zen Masters understood the need to shed all logic and attachment, becoming pure particles of Light. The evolution of Man is not the intellectual and moral betterment of all. It is the liberation from measured Time of the fully detached Master. The fate of all cannot be allowed to hold a Master in mortal bondage. The Master alone is evolution. To evolve is to achieve unity with the holographic Soul. Man has always known he must return to space, project himself OUT, but now we can comprehend that space is emptiness, the edge of a cloud. With our ability to project our Brain via Television, we can behold our final journey. The painted bird flies from the canvas, which was already blank. The great lie has been that we exist. The holographic Soul is a technological development that came when it was needed. There is no reason to fear it, we created it

because we NEED it. Like the electric light. Everybody will want to know about this, and that is proof enough of its importance. It does what every new creation does: it lets a little more Light into the darkness of man, it fills the Brain of Man with more light, and it is the means to be free of Man forever. Out of the confines of the body, out of the chains of the Mind. In Light is meant for those who can let everything GO. The alchemists, the mystics, the holy lunatics, they all understood, they could describe illumination. We can program it. They could touch the state of Liberation, they could taste immortality, but they did not have the computer to contain and mobilize the Soul.

From Kreutzer's Journal
August 5th, 1968

Fugu does not just access alternate realities, it amplifies conclusions.

From Kreutzer's Journal
February 22nd, 1972

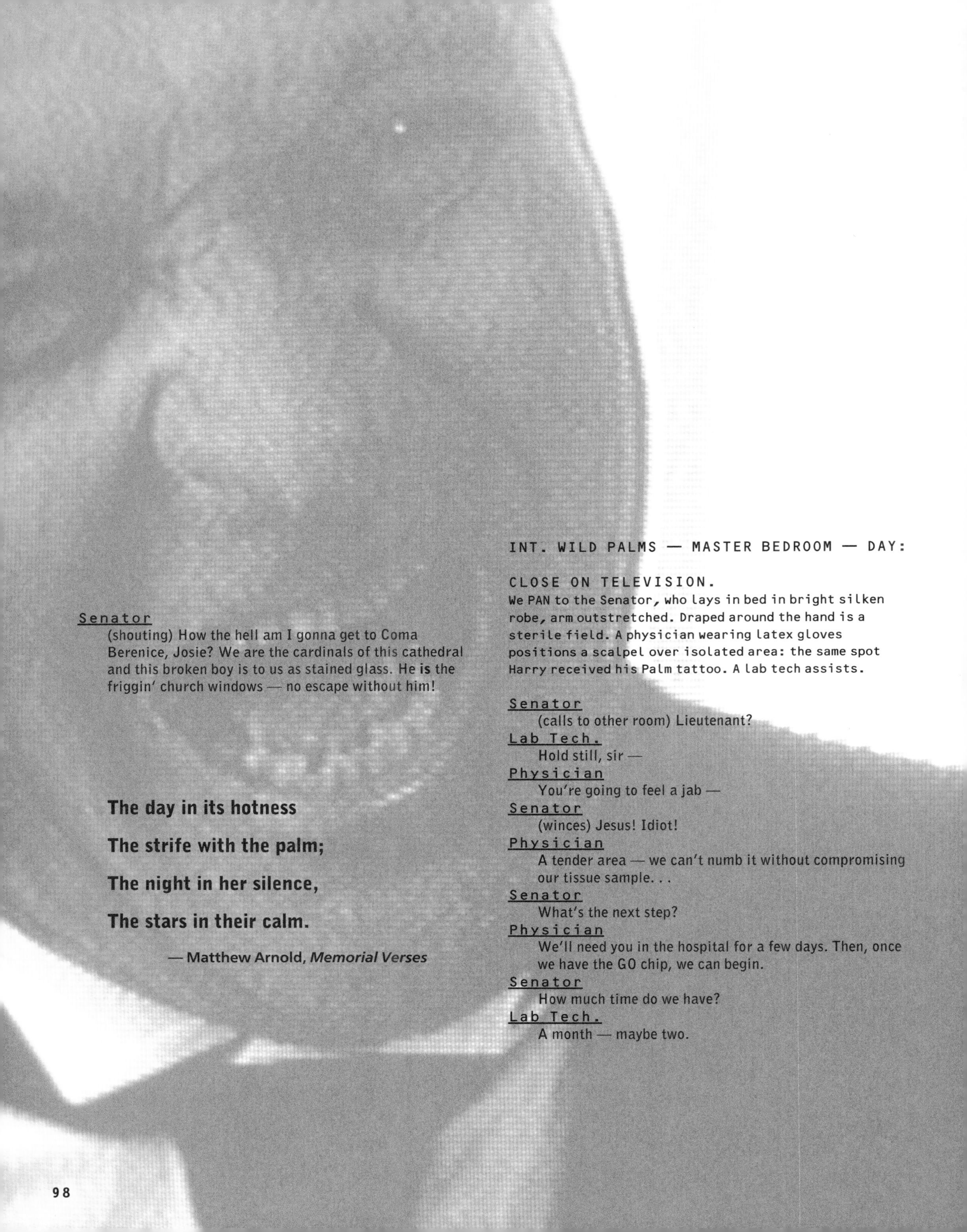

Senator
(shouting) How the hell am I gonna get to Coma
Berenice, Josie? We are the cardinals of this cathedral
and this broken boy is to us as stained glass. He **is** the
friggin' church windows — no escape without him!

The day in its hotness

The strife with the palm;

The night in her silence,

The stars in their calm.

— Matthew Arnold, *Memorial Verses*

INT. WILD PALMS — MASTER BEDROOM — DAY:

CLOSE ON TELEVISION.
We PAN to the Senator, who lays in bed in bright silken
robe, arm outstretched. Draped around the hand is a
sterile field. A physician wearing latex gloves
positions a scalpel over isolated area: the same spot
Harry received his Palm tattoo. A lab tech assists.

Senator
(calls to other room) Lieutenant?
Lab Tech.
Hold still, sir —
Physician
You're going to feel a jab —
Senator
(winces) Jesus! Idiot!
Physician
A tender area — we can't numb it without compromising
our tissue sample. . .
Senator
What's the next step?
Physician
We'll need you in the hospital for a few days. Then, once
we have the GO chip, we can begin.
Senator
How much time do we have?
Lab Tech.
A month — maybe two.

INT. WILD PALMS — GUEST HOUSE — NIGHT:
Chickie sweats in his wheelchair, while Chap directs a light on his "subject."

Chickie
Terra doesn't know anything!

Chap
She's more than just an innocent ballerina. . . That old man in Kyoto shouldn't have betrayed you, Chickie — you could've been back at the beach by now.

Chickie
Ushio didn't betray me!

Chap
Ushio is the ballerina, can't you see that? Ushio's Terra —

Chickie
Liar!

Chap
Talk to me, Chickie! Tell me about the Go chip or Terra's gonna hurt, it's that simple. She's already in pain; don't make it worse. Tell me your secrets. Help the Senator, and Terra will be free. . .

CAMERA PANS TO EXTREME CLOSEUP of Chickie's "eyeglasses" on the bedside table: we see the computer-generated Terra in one of the lenses, her mouth open in a silent scream. She takes a pair of "eiglasses" from table, walks them to Chickie.

Josie
Terra's going to suffer for your cruelties — oh yes. They sent a virus after your fragile black paramour: it'll catch her, and eat her — just like a Grimm's fairy tale! Here — take a look. . .
She put the glasses on his face.

CLOSE ON LENS:
(Terra screaming, MOS.)
We ENTER the Lens: Terra runs for her life, pursued by something bestial.

Grace
They're buying you —

Harry
(irate) What?

Grace
Can't you see what's happening?

Harry
Wait a minute.
(beat)
You wanted this too, remember?

Grace
No, Harry — not this! It's a sham! You don't know how dangerous that man is!

Harry
(sarcastic) Here we go: Senator Tony Kreutzer, big bad bully of the Brave New World. A hard rain's gonna fall — right, Grace? Well, let it!

Grace
I don't know you anymore. . .

Harry
That makes two of us. Why didn't you tell me Eli Levitt was your father?

Grace
I. . . I couldn't —

Harry
Sort of strange, isn't it? Married twelve years and you lie about something like that! What else are you lying about?

Grace
I didn't want to bring you into it — I thought they'd leave us alone. . .

Harry
(almost mocking) 'They'? 'They' who, the Mafia? Did I marry into the Mob, Grace? I mean, who am I supposed to believe? You sit there with your nineteen nervous breakdowns —

Grace
Goddam you! That technology he's developed is addictive—

Harry
Yeah, yeah, they said that about TV fifty years ago — and they were wrong.

Grace
We're not talking Thomas Edison here! One day, in the middle of 'Church Windows,' we'll find our country no longer belongs to us — and no one'll even care! Wild Palms silences their enemies, Harry: with artificial dreams — and real death squads!

Harry
The 'conspiracy from hell.' You know what? Life is a conspiracy, against all of us: you either run for the hills with your tail between your legs — or stick around and fight for the beach house!

Grace
Spoken like a true New Realist.

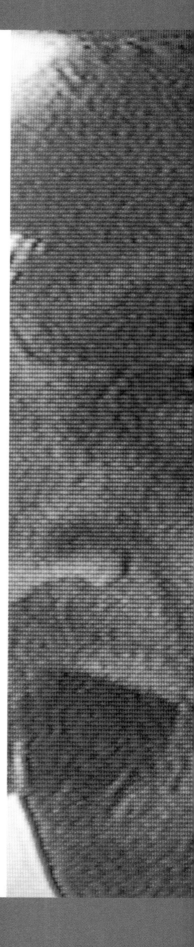

Maps to the Stars

WHAT DOES THE SENATOR WANT ME TO DO?

THE AGENCY'S PACKAGED A FILM, TO STAR TABBA AND YOUR SON, AMONG OTHERS. IT'S A PROFOUNDLY IMPORTANT PROJECT FOR US, AND JOSIE WAS EXEC-PRODUCING BEFORE SHE BECAME ILL. MR. KREUTZER WISHES YOU TO FILL IN.

WHAT'S IT ABOUT?

WELL, ON THE SIMPLEST LEVEL, IT'S ABOUT A BEL AIR WHOREHOUSE—YOU KNOW, FOR ASPIRING STARLETS AND BORED WIVES OF STUDIO EXECUTIVES...

LIKE BELLE DU JOUR—

IF YOU LIKE.

HE WANTS TO CALL IT...MAPS TO THE STARS.

DO THEY HAVE A TITLE?

I WANTED TO CALL IT *THE VARIETIES OF RELIGIOUS EXPERIENCE*, BUT THE SENATOR THOUGHT THAT WAS TOO ARTY. HE'S GOT SOMETHING ELSE IN MIND.

OH?

EXT. WILD PALMS —
TERRACE/ROCK GARDEN —
DAY:

Senator
 Recognize it?
Harry
 (doesn't)
 It's a — a Zen garden...
Senator
 The Zen garden —
Paige
 Ryoanji, in Kyoto.
Senator
 Faithful to the centimeter.
Paige
 Harry said it looks like dogs in the
 water.
Harry
 I was kidding.
Senator
 I love that.
Harry
 Then I wasn't kidding.
Senator
 'He looked at Ryoanji and saw dogs
 in the water.' That's kickass haiku!
Paige
 Anton was going to have the
 real thing brought over, stone by
 stone.
Harry
 Seriously?
Senator
 Damn right. Knew some yakuza
 who'd steal the whole damn
 garden for me.

Senator
 You're going to Kyoto — both of
 you. Right after 'Windows' debuts.
Harry
 Why?
Senator
 There's something I want you to
 pick up — part of the 'Go' game.
 You've played Go, haven't you,
 Harry?
Harry
 As in, 'everything must'?
Senator
 (laughs, exits)
 Paige is a helluva guide — she'll
 show you the tao — I'm not talkin'
 Dow Jones!

Suddenly he reaches over and tears off
Harry's bandage; the Senator's demeanor
changes from reflective to wild-eyed.
Harry stands; Paige appears nervously in
b.g.

Senator
What did they give you in Kyoto?
Harry
What are you talking about?
Senator
Was it the GO chip, Harry?
Harry
No —
Senator
Ushio gave it to you, he said so! Why
would he lie?
Harry
I don't know —
Senator
Would you betray me, Harry?
Harry
No!
Senator
Would you keep me from eternity? Why
did you go to the doctor?
Harry
I had a cyst removed —
Senator
Is that what eternity is? A **cyst?**

The Senator grabs Harry and
kisses him, Godfather-style.
The kiss of death. Men in suits appear.

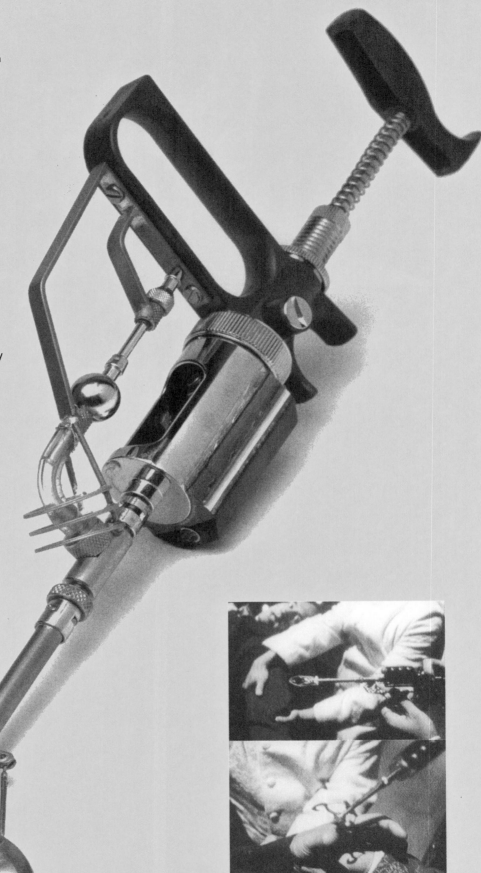

Eli stands, goes to her, lifts her from chair —
she's helpless. He kisses her deeply.

Eli
    Release Chickie — or there's nothing to talk about.

This time, she kisses him — hungrily.

Josie
    I'll give you Chickie. . .
    (more kisses)
    for Grace.
    He smiles at her, sly. She smiles back. He kisses her
    then bites her lip. She screams, stumbling away in
    pain. He moves on her, grabs her; whispers intently in
    her ear as she cringes at his words.

Eli
    You're no general! You're a mercenary — a cannibal!
    A pimp, with the wings of a bat! I never wanted you —
    any part of you!
    Bloodied and humiliated, she storms from the pool.

Josie
    SUBTITLED Japanese:
    You will pay! You will pay!

EXT. BEACH — DAY
The van pulls onto sand. Eli and Paige carry Chickie
to water, leaving behind the wailing Tommy.

Eli
    We're here, baby boy! See? We're at the water. . .
Chickie
    It's real?
Eli
    (crying)
    Remember how Mama always brought you the ocean
    when you got sick?
Chickie
    (crying)
    Where's the orchestra?
    (as Paige watches, crying softly now)
    I hear a symphony —

He dies. Eli howls to the skies with rage and
horror as he holds him — a *Pieta*.

104

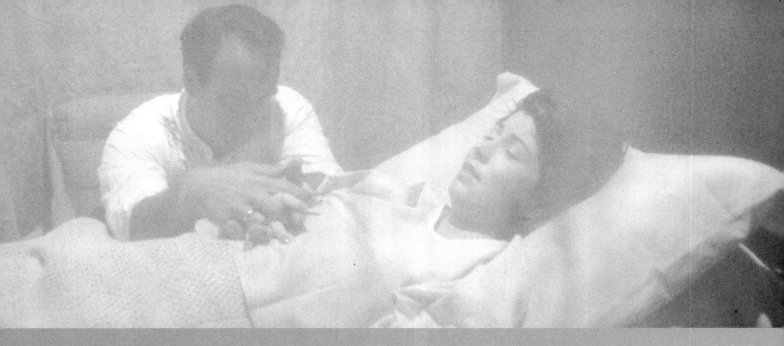

I see them now, their pale, translucent faces gathered 'round me. They are all here: friends, lovers, betrayers, victims — all of them here with me, but I know they are not real. I am an addict, a junkie — I can't seem to live a moment without the sweet, deadly scenes playing out in my head, again and again. Always the same props: blood, steel, a branch of cherry blossoms. Only the players change — sometimes it's Coty, sometimes Harry, or Mother, or Ito, sometimes I can't even see the face. And then sometimes it's me. A knife, a sword, a gun. Death. Deirdre calls to me, "Come to me, Mother, come save me!"

Deirdre, Little Buddha — can you speak? Then tell me what you see with your dark, mournful eyes? How I miss your silence! The memory of your grave, gentle moon of a face moves me as no words can. If I had been able to speak the truth, you would still be here with me. I could have taught you a language that meant something. How long I waited to hear you say "Mama" or "Daddy." Now I don't even know if those words are true. No wonder you disdained them! Whose daughter am I? Whose wife? Whose mother? Am I real, or am I —

I hear her calling me. I know her voice is false. But what does it matter? My voice has been false, too, all these years.

All these years. . . I knew everything! More than Josie, more than Eli, more than the Senator. I saw the faces behind the masks, but they never made an impression on me. I always preferred the glamorous, changeable facade to the naked truth — I have too much God-damned fashion sense.

It's amazing I've lived this long, amazing they've let me. "Weak dog!" Mother called me, and she was right. They were so sure of me — of my weakness, of my silence, of my selfish, vain humility.

They were sure of me because they knew what I wanted, which was no more than my megalo-maniacal bloodlines would allow — no more,

but no less. Oh, I wanted to be small and meek, yes, to lead an ordinary life. What I wanted was nothing much — nothing more than eternal love and happiness!

And I paid for it. When I kept the truth from Harry I thought I was protecting him. Now I have killed him, as I have killed everyone I love, as surely as if I had planted a bomb. It is twilight, and we are dying, all of us, half-dead, flickering in and out, wandering aimlessly now, circling, scratching, shadows looking for a place to lie down. Maybe I could have saved the world from itself if I'd taken the risk. If I'd spoken the truth.

Maybe. But who would I have told? Who would have believed me?

Not the hungry ghosts. We are all ghosts now. Me, Harry, Coty — yes, even you, Little Buddha, dear, false baby girl. What will become of us when there are no more of the living left to haunt? Will we turn and devour each other — or will we devour ourselves? A suicidal orgy to carry us into a brave new world where the skin is the new frontier — beyond it lie unexplored galaxies of blood and bone. What I need now is a Big Bang.

Then silence.

My silent child, perhaps you are right to refuse speech. Words are useless, now that our race has learned to lie with flesh and blood, with holograms and hallucinogens. If you are alive — if you live — you will inherit a world that melts on the tongue. A world where experiences leave us shaking and weak and hungry the morning after. A world where reality is a pose. A world where blood is nothing but a pretty color. Look, darling, just look at all the pretty colors!

I love you! Do you hear me? Can you see me? I don't know, Little Buddha, I just don't have the answers anymore — I used to, but it is too late for all that, too late. I have answers, yes — but where are the questions?

In this world of pretty colors, all is silent.

And love — perhaps you have no use for love. What color is love? I don't know. All I can tell you is that it is hot, and wet, and that it spills from my heart, even as I die.

Senator

An unstable woman. . . that kind of
hysteria is often contagious. Divorce
her, Harry — make it official;
unburden yourself.
(beat)
Wild Palms has big plans, and
you're a part of them.
Everything's got to run smoothly
now. Is my marriage to Paige going
to be a problem?

Harry

Why should it?

Senator

It's tough to put out an old flame.
(beat)
I withheld certain things from you
because you would not **understand**.
Nothing 'Machiavellian' about it.

Harry

I know that.

Senator

I am leaving this earth, Harry —
taking a full crew with me. That has
been my life's work. You're either
onboard — or behind, with the
scum.

Harry

I'm with you — let me be like a son.

Senator

Talk to the boy — talk to Coty.
(embraces Harry)
'For this, thy brother was dead, and
is alive again; and was lost, and is
found.'

IT'S YOUR SON, HARRY. HE'S GOT SECRETS TO REVEAL. GET IN.

Man gave names in order to control. To reduce, to comprehend the forces of nature, to demonstrate ownership. In this race to name, the poor have grown to be rich, and the rich have grown to be poor again. The New Realist knows that to re-enter immortality we must ourselves become unnameable, emptied of all sense of being here.

The end of Time is just another way of saying the beginning of Immortality.

— Anton Kreutzer, *Wild Psalms*

EXTERIOR. PRIVATE
HOSPITAL. NIGHT:
Candlelight vigil. Coty
addresses the acolytes.

Coty
    Poor men have grown to be rich men. . .
    and rich men grown to be poor again.
ALL
    And I am running to Paradise.
Coty
    The wind is old and still at play, While
    I must hurry upon my way. . .
ALL
    For I am running to Paradise. . .

EXTERIOR. PRIVATE
HOSPITAL. NIGHT:
As the Senator listens through the open
window, his eyes look skyward...

Senator
    Soon. . . soon. . . soon. . .

RB Donner
School of Oriental and African Studies
University of London
London, England
November 2, 2008

Dear Mr. Truman,

Although I have been an avid reader of DETAILS for some time, I found the recent parallelling of Senator Kreutzer to Goethe's *Faust* somewhat overdrawn — indeed, almost Woiwodean. Rather, I believe the Senator to be far more indebted to the Eastern alchemical tradition, whose purpose is summed up in the phrase "to make of the body a spirit and of the spirit a body." Could there be any more apt description of the logic and method of Channel 3?

While Western alchemy has traditionally focused on transformation (i.e. from lead into gold), in China the Elixir of Immortality was always the primary alchemical objective. Its effects were to so rarify the body that it could fly through the air, assume transparency or invisibility, penetrate solids, "become many" — that is, be several places at once —and enter other men's minds. Alchemically speaking, such objectives might apply to Kreutzer's books but a little, and to his business alot.

One need look little further than to one of the Senator's best-known metaphors to see the influence of Eastern alchemy: his likening of the television set to that Japanese household shrine thought to hold the "tamashi," or life-force, of the family. Is this not like that "reverted Elixir" which, when placed in a heated container "even while you are watching, will suddenly glow and sparkle with all the colors of divine light?" A Controller of Recipes advised the Emperor Wu that he "should worship the Stove, and then you can make spiritual beings present themselves."

You liken the Senator to Faust, but the best efforts of all the Eli Levitts in the world have so far brought forth no Mephistophelian aroma from the Senator's corner. And indeed, what need would he have for the Devil when he has the resources of Mimecom to search for the Elixir?

The parallels with mimezine are not idle ones. Powdered rhino horn was considered an essential ingredient of the Elixir, which was also said to produce the sensation of insects crawling on one's skin — a classic entactogenic symptom it shares with the *fugu*-derived chemistry said to be at the root of mimezine.

Far more certain is their similarity of effect, including time-loss — i.e. "dreaming awake," or lucid dreaming — and the ability to "make everyone see mountains moving and trees transporting themselves, though no actual movement takes place."

Of course, the briefest reflection on those thousands addicted to the black market variants of mimezine is also long enough to make us appreciate its differences from the Elixir. After all, what could be worse than this plague of junkies? Only a plague of immortal junkies.

I believe that the Senator is determined to achieve some variant of the Elixir, and perhaps his enemies can hope for nothing better than that he succeed. For as Professor Cooper has written, "Alchemy aims at death, or total transformation, which is the same thing." Or as Ko Hung put it, "Those wishing to enter the path of geniehood are as numerous as the hairs on a buffalo, while the successful are as rare as the horn of the unicorn."

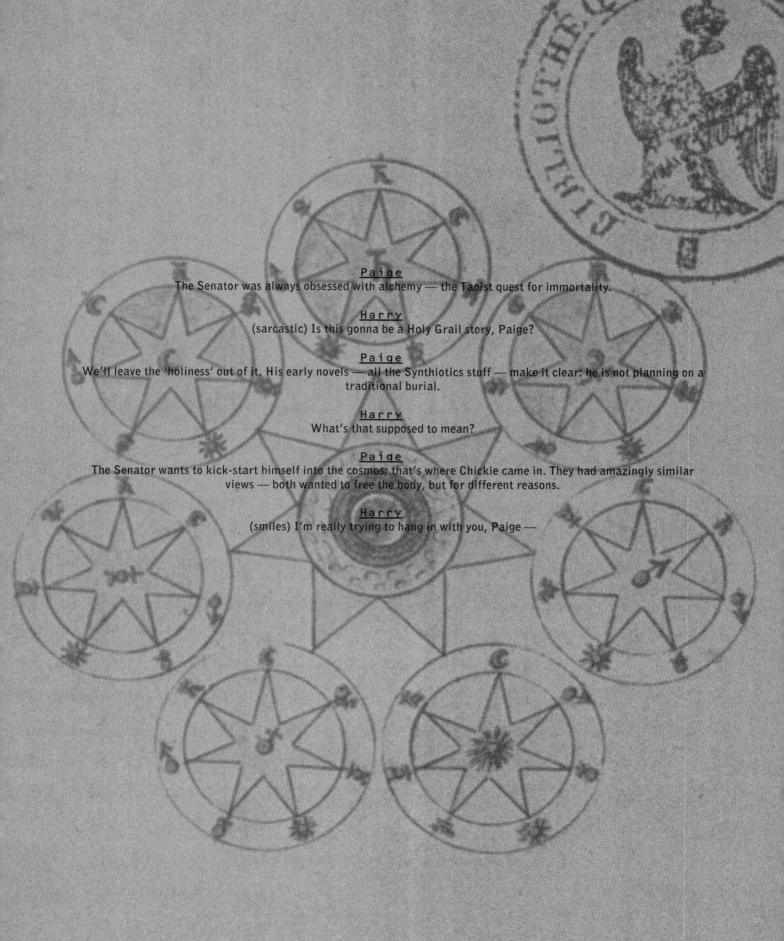

Paige
The Senator was always obsessed with alchemy — the Taoist quest for immortality.

Harry
(sarcastic) Is this gonna be a Holy Grail story, Paige?

Paige
We'll leave the 'holiness' out of it. His early novels — all the Synthiotics stuff — make it clear: he is not planning on a traditional burial.

Harry
What's that supposed to mean?

Paige
The Senator wants to kick-start himself into the cosmos; that's where Chickie came in. They had amazingly similar views — both wanted to free the body, but for different reasons.

Harry
(smiles) I'm really trying to hang in with you, Paige —

To: Wild Palms Complex, Rancho Mirage CA

From: Kansas State Perceptory, Kansas City KS

In the course of our research into brain death, cellular mortality, and the biology of consciousness, we have been attempting to determine the chemical effects of neurochip implants. Now we see that we may have stumbled onto — or into — some sort of alternative to biological dying. We hope the Senator's confidence in our way of doing things will be reinforced.

Were this a Pharm, the constraints would be far too great. However, with such a large pool of "mental patients" to draw from, all of whom have been certified as criminally insane, we've been able to experiment freely, and thus make progress more quickly. (And for their part, it behooves the inmates here to cooperate. After all, if the experiments work, they might actually get out. They think.)

As you know, we have been working extensively with empathogens, that is, with drugs that affect the physical interface of perception. The way to change people's ideas about reality is to change the way they feel reality — literally. If we're going to tinker with reality as it has always been known, we have to have a solid concept of the biology and chemistry involved.

Since prior experiments with empathogens seemed promising, we upped the dosage of the empathogen to a full one-third, toned down the hypnotic, and beefed up the hallucinogen. (Once the GO chip has been refined, perhaps we can tone down the hallucinogen again — or maybe we'll have to use even more of it, depending on how texture-rich the results are.

Perhaps it will take a strong dose of hallucinogen to help the acclimation to a brave new reality.)

Then we took two groups of the most troublesome of the political prisoners, the dosed group and the control group, and as usual followed double-blind procedures.

Every one of the subjects receiving the mixture reported a very intense hallucinatory experience. But for one — call her Subject Y — the episode was especially significant. She suffered a seizure and then went into cardiac arrest, remaining dead for a total of twenty minutes before our medical emergency team was able to revive her.

We had thought that, due to the seizure, she would not even remember receiving the drug. But as it turns out, she not only remembers what happened before she died, she remembers what happened *after*.

The excerpt below is from the transcript of our post-experiment interview with Subject Y. Was it an experience real only to her, or was it a real experience? We think the former led into and became the latter, something that has a great deal of bearing on the GO chip project.

Q. *Do you remember feeling anything strange before you had the seizure*?
A. What do you think? [pause; then, more quietly] Yeah. Yeah. I could actually feel how the drug was travelling through my circulatory system. I knew when it went through my arms and legs and my heart and all. I could feel it rising up into my head. You know how it feels to sink down real slow into water and have it go over your head? Well, it was a lot like that, but inside.
Q. *After you lost consciousness, did —*
A. I *didn't* lose consciousness. I died, but I was

conscious the whole time. Believe me, I know this.

Q. *Well, then, can you tell us what happened?*

A. [long pause] I can tell you what I did. I walked out of this room and into another. [pause] Don't look around like that, I don't mean that kind of room. I mean *this here*, where we are now — this world, this . . . what do you guys keep calling it, this reality — is one room, and I stepped into another. I slipped away. I wanted to. I didn't want to die, but I wanted to leave. This was the only way. As I moved into that . . . room, I could feel how all this [gestures with arms] had been all over me, like a wrapping, or a — a casing. And I just slipped out of it into somewhere else. You didn't have me any more.

Q. *Just like that?*

A. Well no, not just like that. I did have to go down this connecting hallway —

Q. *The tunnel with the bright light at the end? Many Near-Death Experience survivors report this.*

A. [pause] No . . . no tunnel. A, a — hallway. I don't know what else to call it. I just got up, walked through this hallway, and into this other room. I know, because I could feel my feet on every step, you know? You know how there are certain things you walk on, certain kinds of surfaces, and you feel all the bones and muscles in the bottom of your feet? I felt that, and I could feel how my legs were moving. Then I could feel my arms swinging and my chest and shoulders, and finally my head and neck. And then I realized that this was my new body.

Q. *Your "new body"?*

A. Right. My new post-life body. Now I'm a ghost.

Q. *Now you're a ghost? Or you were a ghost then?*

A. No. *Now* I'm a ghost. If you people would just do the decent thing and let go of me, I could go back to being alive.

Q. *What?*

A. [getting impatient] By calling me back, you've turned me into a ghost. Which is only logical because I died. But then you had to go bringing me back, and it's very unnatural. I belong over there now, in the other room. Because I'm dead. Relatively.

Q. *You're relatively dead?*

A. Relative to here, yeah. In the new room, I'm not dead. It's not that I'm *alive*, just that it's something totally different over there. [pause] I belong there, now, not here. All this [wipes hands over self], all this is wrong, it doesn't fit right any more. I don't belong here any more. I don't fit. I don't fit!

(end excerpt)

Subject Y's conviction that she is dead, a ghost relative to this world and alive somewhere else, would be classified as a post-traumatic delusion, except for the length of time Subject Y was deceased with no ill effects.

We know that this is not exactly what the Senator had in mind. But it's a start! We die because we have no choice — now we may have a choice! The results of this experiment can be replicated. At the moment, we are running tests designed to measure and profile Subject Y down to the finest detail. What in her brain chemistry was amenable to the post-death experience, and how can we recreate it in other brains? And does that chemistry have to exist before the drug is administered?

Obviously, we've just got to get this dosage right. It's going to take a lot of time and resources, but thanks to the Fathers, we probably won't run short of either . . .

[end]

DREAM

2008

In a world that is becoming a hologram, a transmitted projection of material 'reality,' he who comprehends the final transmission controls all projections, controls the world, and controls the secret of the identity and malleability of corporeal matter. For anything, any cherished belief, adhered to and given mythic form by the masses, becomes manifestly solid, and tangible. What we believe in all ways comes to pass. Nothing can exist that we do not believe in. At these times consciousness is not centered in the world of form, it is experiencing the world of content. The prophet will become king. Any ability to cope with the world of form and there create order is a measure of insanity, a poor connection between Mind and Brain, which must become one autonomous program, globally transmitted, to generate its own liberation from form in the mass political hallucination that makes the master become the final reality, transcending time, body and place.

— From Kreutzer's Journal
January 17th 1968

All Hallucinations are Real. Some Hallucinations are more Real than others.

— From Kreutzer's Journal
August 5th 1967

Memo: 1:
Public E-Mail Key: 23-89654-00
Private E-Mail Key: xx-xxxx-xx
From: turner@mimecom. kyoto. com (Athanasius Turner, Chief Realitech, First-Tier Synthiotician)
To: all@synthlabs.wildpalms.org (Synthiotics Perception Labs Personnel)
Date: Sat, 29 Aug 2008 17:14:00 PDT

Orange Book Security:
Synthiotics First Tier — Eyes Only

The Great Text states:

"Our journey centers around *perception* as the new organizing commodity of society. Our seizure of the *means of perception* does not merely complement financial capital, but renders capital, and capitalism itself, utterly irrelevant" (*On The Way To The Garden 23:14*).

Senator Kreutzer's historic conceptual breakthrough, so brilliantly limned in the prescient *Garden*, is no mere theory of pubic relations. Nor is it a theory of advertising or account control — although it does help explain their ascendancy in the post-symbolic Information Society.

Today, with the successful manufacture here in Kyoto of the GO molecular-processor nanochip, we at last stand on the brink of the grand transmutation. Senator Kreutzer's theory, expressed decades ago in a work once improperly dismissed as "science fiction," will be made *flesh*. The time has come for all properly cleared Synthioticians to consider the true meaning of this statement, the deep implications of our own ambitions.

Those of us who have achieved the rank of First Tier in Synthiotics, to whom responsibility has properly been granted, those of us who hold the *cutting edge* in our hands — we must not and we shall not flinch. I want to take the opportunity today to state the implications of our aims quite boldly.

Our success necessarily means the entire destruction of America's current financial and political order.

This is only to be expected — and welcomed. The lines along which the United States Constitution was drafted — the halting, pre-industrial social theory of Locke and Jefferson — warped and vanished long ago into the shimmering haze of digital postmodernity. Concepts such as "freedom of the press" had *already* vanished, even before the metal "press" — and the print-era lords of the press — both became dead-tech anachronisms. Freedom from search and seizure vanished decades ago, during the drug wars. The doctrine of habeas corpus fell victim to the Boca Raton atrocity. Various forms of confidentiality — of lawyer-client, analyst-patient, spouse-to-spouse, Fifth Amendment protection from self-incrimination, the privacy of medical, financial, and tax records — simply no longer exist in today's Information Society.

Even the most extraordinary police powers have not been able to restrain the resultant violent outbreak of warlordism, as various American power-groups, marooned by the destruction of civil society, defend themselves from one another by essentially feudal measures: fortress security, assassination, kidnapping, and heavily armed private militia.

As a political entity and social commonwealth, the United States of America was long ago severed from its conceptual roots. The State of the Founding Fathers simply withered and died, the mummified facade slowly flaking away to reveal the essential savagery of our harsh new age. For decades — during the entire lifetime of most of you who are reading this electronic missive — America as a cultural entity has been a blundering patchwork Frankenstein in a multivalent, zombified, chaotic random-walk. America's cultural leaders are all for sale, its artists and even its religious leaders the complete pawns of the forces of marketing, global merchantry, and commodity exchange. And America's federal government has been in the hands of panic-stricken astrologers since 1980.

To quote the Senator's favorite poet, Yeats: "The best lack all conviction, while the worst are filled with passionate intensity." The gigantic cultural engine that is

Virtual America spins at random, roaring and emitting a foul smoke. Vibrating violently, it loops and spins in the dark pull of its strange attractor — when those energies might be *harnessed*.

The United States of America will be the first society to be actually *swallowed* by its own technology — by the ontological transcendence inherent in the American-spawned information media. This has probably been America's destiny — what our Kansai friends might call America's karma — ever since the American polity first created the telegraph and telephone. The Revolution eats its children, and even the crude analog web of Alexander Bell's telephone had a technological impetus sufficient to circle and enshroud the entire planet.

Today, in the new millennium, America spins headlong at the very brink of a dark vortex of digital virtuality. America can, and will, and must, *vanish entirely* into that vortex. And Wild Palms Group will be the eye of that vortex — the eye of the post-symbolic storm.

With the Agricultural Revolution, mankind seized the means of organic production. With the Industrial Revolution, we seized the means of mechanical production. With the Information Revolution we seized the means of symbolic production. But the postsymbolic Virtual Revolution is far more profound than any of these earlier disruptions, for it seizes the means of perception itself — the very means of *cognition*. Through the GO Chip™ and Mimezine® it now becomes possible to actually *interrupt the stream of human consciousness*, and indeed to divert the enormous power of that stream to our own specific ends. The deepest reservoirs of human perception and consciousness can be diverted at will, changing the old patterns of consciousness with the McLuhanesque abruptness of a station-break for commercials — or a thumb on the remote-control.

Today the new technology stands ready to surge through New Millennium America like one vast sheet of lightning. I know that some of you, especially the junior officers, may doubt this. It will be asked within the councils of Synthiotics (and it has been asked) how a Radio Shack unit retailing for under a thousand dollars can possibly match the results we here at the Kyoto labs have attained with Mr. Levitt's high-end virtuality equipment. This skepticism within our organization is understandable — and as your chief technical officer I stand ready to answer all objections.

The processing through-rate that Chickie Levitt has achieved — some eighty million polygons a second — is indeed very technically impressive. The software algorithms he created to handle those polygons is an even more profound achieve-ment. But a throughput of this scale requires the bandwidth of a backbone fiber-optic cable from a national research network — not the thin bandwidth of cable TV or worse yet, broadcast. However, we *can* take Levitt's conceptual breakthroughs and scale them down to the level of commercial televised applications. It is no different in principle than the transition of processing power from the mainframe to the desktop.

The human mind does not perceive, and never has perceived, reality as "polygons," eighty million or no. Repeated perceptual tests prove that the human mind derives its impression of so-called "reality" through an astonishingly narrow and data-poor series of quick retinal impressions. This very limited visual tracking — commonly, only ten to fifteen percent of our environment is ever subjected to a direct focus by the eyeball — is assembled into a seamless *perception* of reality by the optic center of the brain (assisted by neural-net subprocessing in the retina and optic nerve.) And these human, organic, wetware visual processors, like all processors, can be "hacked."

Thanks to the new fractal compression techniques perfected by Mimecom Kyoto, it is entirely possible to cram *more detail* into an image than was *present in the original image itself*. There is no "image degradation" when one

G o

uses fractal compression — quite the opposite, for the more the image is fractally manipulated, the more apparently "real" it becomes! Thanks to its dedicated fractal-processor math-chip, the cheap, affordable Mimecom Adaptor can create cheap, mass-produced holo imagery. And this *fractal* imagery possesses a virtual and underscore perceptual *density* that no merely natural object can possibly rival!

Of course, fractally generated detail is not "accurate" detail, in the sense that it is not "true to the original" — as if that mattered! "Real" detail would require enormous processing power. The density of fractal detail is *mathematically generated*, right on the spot, in every living room in America, in a matter of microseconds, from a quite unexceptional sixth-generation math chip.

"Is it real, or is it Mimecom?" The slogan, while truly brilliant on a commercial level, is technologically irrelevant. The Mimecom image is, simply *better* than real — and the human mind senses this on an entirely unconscious level. Despite the quite thin bandwidth of modern-day TV broadcast, our fractally assisted, digitized Mimecom holography carries a neural "impression" of authenticity that overwhelms the human brain's own perceptual centers! Any doubts simply *fade into the algorithm* on an entirely unconscious, organic, cellular level.

Mimezine-dosed volunteers have been scanned with EEGs, magnetic resonance imaging, and computer-ized axial tomography. The nature of the effects are no longer in doubt. Granted, there is indication that prolonged exposure to mimezine can cause the brain to purge the neurons of certain synaptic neurotransmitters. And yes, the resultant osmotic pressure can result in a distressing leakage of bluish lymph from the nose. We admit this frankly — and we move ahead. *All* drugs have side effects, especially in large doses. *Fugu* toxin, the parent neurochemical of mimezine, is lethal. Mimezine is *not a toy*. It is a *tool* that can be used to topple the cosmos.

This is in some sense the true "last secret" — not that "secrets" themselves are "impossible" per se in an Information Society, but that the entire ontological structure of Cartesian doubt has been rendered irrelevant by Synthiotic Science. "Secrets" are meaningless. Plotting is meaningless, paranoia is meaningless, conventional politics is utterly meaningless, and the entire desperate order of our quotidian lives can be circumvented at a stroke.

Even the squalid nuclear butchery that was Boca Raton can no longer lie on the national conscience like some tormenting incubus. It no longer matters who killed Kennedy, who invented AIDS, who sent the earthquakes, who took the children, who crashed the banking system, who killed Boca Raton. We, the Synthioticians, can now directly engineer the fundamental cosmic constants of life and thought — matters that were once merely tortuously debated by the likes of Berkeley and Wittgenstein. With the use of mimezine to enhance the effect, our physical command over the means of perception and cognition are complete.

The matter, the responsibility, is grave, but it must be faced directly, today and in the very short future. Relying entirely on the Synthiotic discipline, we must watch with utter alertness, with our eyes, and our nerves wide open — as all that is solid melts into air.

And once we ourselves have melted, *why stay here?* What, besides simple inertia and fear, ties us to this squalid, wrecked, polluted and corrupted corner of cosmic space-time? We enter the Theatre of All Possibilities. We cross Tomorrow's Bridge. It is the great consummation at last. And it lies within our hands.

As our friends — our partners — here in Kyoto say, "To eat *fugu* is foolish. But **not** to eat *fugu* is *also* foolish." I have seen the future, ladies and gentlemen — and it is Channel 3.

J. Athanasius Turner, Ph. D.VOX
(075) 771-6111
Mimecom LabsFAX (075) 751-1196
Heian Bunka Center
Okazaki, Sakyo-ku
Kyoto 606, NIPPON
turner@mimecom.kyoto.com
". . . a magnificent atavism — the remnant of ecstatic myth"
OTWITG 45:92

EXTERIOR. METROPOLITAN
DETENTION CENTER. DAY:
The press await. Josie EXITS
building and descends steps,
flanked by Attorney and men in
suits.

First Reporter
    Why'd you kill her, Josie?
Second Reporter
    How'd you make bail?
Josie
    I didn't kill anyone.
Attorney
    That was a doctored tape — a
    fabrication!
Second Reporter
    Is your brother going to choose a
    new running mate?
Third Reporter
    Will he drop out of the
    campaign?
Josie
    Absolutely not! Why should he?
Third Reporter
    What's your defense going to be?
Attorney
    Not guilty!
First Reporter
    But the whole country saw you
    murder your daughter. Seeing is
    believing.
Josie
    (withering) You must be kidding.

Tobias
The Senator will be remembered as a cosmic Don Quixote.

Josie
All he wanted to do was escape his miserable childhood. Can anyone begrudge him that?

Tobias
I talked to him an hour ago — he still thinks he's going 'to the place where holograms when you turn off the TV.'
(Laughs, kisses her neck)
I'm afraid it's a case of the Emperor's new mind.

Josie
Stranger things have happened.

Tobias
True — for example, did you know the entire universe started off no larger than the head of a pin?

Josie
(lecherous) The Big Bang.

Tobias
It began as a tiny little speck: infinitely hot, infinitely dense. . .

I lay in the desert, on my back, staring up at the stars. I could feel millions of rays of light entering my body, one from each star, infinite numbers, my cell walls broke down, my sense of bodily existence ended, I was illumination, a 3D projection of cosmic light, I could see the ancient shamans building sacred sites to fix their relationship with the descriptions of white light, the myths and legends of our descent from the stars. I was not corporeal, I was a mirage, scaled within an inherited apparently solid body by the weight of History, and by the weight of Fear and Guilt. I shimmered like a ghost, ectoplasm, illusion, and all the puzzles I had heard in Japan, and all the limited descriptions of limitless transcendent experiences made sense. I knew I had to find a way to GO, to leave this sealed coffin that is my body, to find an accelerator to project my brain, bypassing the tedium of mechanistic evolution, into deepest omniversal space, into immortality, into the very fabric of myth and heaven. I was everyone, everything, and everything too was here to GO I understood my lifetime's sense of discon-nection/disorder was not a flaw, rather a wondrous gift that described in a new way, the true nature of being that may be experience whilst trapped, mortal, and confused, here in this desert that was once a theater of all possibilities, and an exit to all impossibilities.

— From Kreutzer's Journal
August 5th 1968

Coty
Are you really going to the place where holograms go?
(The Senator nods)
But you're not going to die!

Senator
Nope — gonna be Emperor of the air.

Coty
The GO chip's taking you?

Senator
They'll put it. . .
(touches the back of his own head) here. The memory of my body, the cathedral of my atoms and my life, will flow into it like water caught in a bowl. Then the bowl will be spilled into space. . . irradiated to Coma Berenices!

Senator (V.O.)
Harry is that you?

Harry sees the Senator, against the far wall. He sits at a little desk, facing the wall, shrouded in darkness.

Harry
Yes, Senator. It's me...

Senator
I knew you were coming — that's why I sent them all away.

Harry
I came for Deirdre.

Senator
I want to thank you for the GO chip. Sorry about all the confusion — it seems Josie and Tobias had other plans. They meant well...

Paige
(behind Harry, whispering) Something's wrong with him.

Senator
Some hours ago, I underwent the procedure...

Harry
How do you feel?

Senator
Well... I'm not sure the GO chip's all what it was trumped up to be. I'm starting to wonder if Chickie Levitt had the last laugh, after all. He just might be up there somewhere, shouting: Do not pass "go"!
(laughs) Do not collect $200 —

Senator
Do you know what the unicorn does when it's surrounded by hunters, Harry?

Harry
Answer me, you psychotic sonofabitch!

Senator
It somersaults into the nearest abyss, breaking the fall with its horn...

The Senator's image begins to WAFFLE — we realize he is a HOLO. Paige and Harry are in shock; the Senator remains rather calm.

Paige
NO!

Harry
What's happening!

Senator
I'm losing focus...

Harry
(agitated) Senator?

Senator
You know, we couldn't exactly predict what would happen... seems I'm not going to make it, Harry —

119

Still tied to the world
I cool off and lose
my form

[As the world already knows, the death-soliloquy of Senator Anton Kreutzer was dutifully recorded by the sleepless circuitry of Wild Palms, whose sentient walls had ears but ironically, no eyes. The bootlegged tape's zealous exegesis has been thorough — so thorough that by now, we know even the minutiae by rote. The editors herewith sacrifice the reader's attention to service the structural integrity of this slim volume.

After his disappearance, Kreutzer's study became a mecca of investigatory bodies. What wasn't destroyed or pirated by New Realist loyalists has been annotated and catalogued, consigned to one hundred years of federal solitude. The Senator cagily remains out of reach.]

oh no . . . No, no. Mistake! *A simple mistake*. Fuck of Jesus — error of my ways. *Terror of my days*. Simple error! Simplicissimus . . . [half-sings, laughs] *Mommy, can you rear me?* [inaudible singing, then] *taking her children away, because they said she was not a good mother . . .*[1] Cunty, wobbling little — [inaudible] *hap-hap-hap-hap-happy talk! talk about things you like to — if you don't have a dream . . .* [inaudible] simplicissimus terror of my days! [singing] *And I am telling you, I'm not going!*[2] [He] repeated himself each and every moment of each and every day, crummy little Hayakawa thoughts and actions, *shit* mundane rituals, even best purest improvised unneurotic moments, *repeated* himself: waking, wailing, puking, sleeping, sucking, in fornications and filigreed monstrous dalliances, even nightly *dreamings* — all threw down and *wallowed* in holy day-in day-outness, so *gaily*, unbelievable, his closely watched middle-class habits, each dribbling from his prick worshipped like big genius miracle, seventy-one white-haired years of it, enough: *true horror lying in his animal enjoyment of said repetition*: hell beyond Sade's wildest imaginings! [inaudible, then

sings] *betcha by golly wow, you're the one that I've been waiting for . . . forever*[3] [inaudible] — *so peaceful here, no one standing over my shoulder, nobody breathing in my ear*[4] [inaudible] [and you] know, Siggy, what matters? I mean, with the dope — after the dope?[5] [coughing jag] Paige and Coty? [inaudible, coughing] [just?] another *car* wreck, that's all *they* are. Shoot me up, you [inaudible] . . . yeah yeah shoot it, kike! Then put it in the hole[6] with Harry's whines and whistles. [I am] not your President, never was. Whose fault is this, anyway? Hey: [sings, laughing] *blame it on the sons, the sons that didn't shine* [inaudible] — *Here's* who I am, then: willful blond locomotive, running along the beach, so very Jeff Chandler — *funky see funky do!* — togging toward said Yid palace built there, consortium of rough yearnings, played out, wild-eyed, quasi-brazen, gargoyle-gravid, a [colon] of redress, *shit* cologne, roaring, charm-braceleted, shamanized, stuporous [tape runs out]

1. Lou Reed, "The Kids", *Berlin*

2. *Dreamgirls*

3. Stylistics, "Betcha By Golly Wow"

4. Helen Reddy, "Peaceful"

5. Sig Kraus, Kreutzer's personal physician

6. In the last months of his life, Kreutzer developed a mania for probing his urethra with foreign bodies. He would also catheterize himself, using the tube as a conduit for drugs, in this case, probably mimezine.

The joy of dewdrops
in the grass as they
turn back to vapor

I borrow moonlight
for this journey of a
million miles

Where the Holograms GO:

Chap Starfall
sings
Chickie's Song

(found in the trunk of an industrial-yellow DeLorean)

CHICKIE: *When will they let me GO, Chap?*

Time to go now. Adios. Goodbye. Pray all are broken, here.

Curbside service in the rain. Maps to the stars. The Senator knew, but he couldn't GO. With the chip in his flesh, his golden arm, palm at the end of the sleeve, he couldn't GO.

Chickie's wheels, down the Sunset sidewalk. Gray rubber. Ghost of his Harris tweed jacket. *Every single surface* is a fractal zoom. Chickie's GO now, and his song goes something like:

Leave this place. Leave it.
Drive a long, long way.

And Chickie will tell you, if you didn't know, that there are suites up in the Marmont where you wouldn't want to go. Not ever. Rooms ritually sealed, thrice concealed, by the Fathers. And there are things up in the

hills. Fires where there shouldn't be, ever. There are dead men in Book Soup, just before it closes.

And Chickie, paralyzed, smiles his last half-smile, as his gray wheels carry him deeper into lines of an increasingly pure geometry. Between vertical planes grown abruptly abstract, playroom planes of shadow-play, walls of Pure Television. And every pixel is a life. A soul. A moment in the dance.

At the point, forever (it must seem) receding, where the planes converge, there is something bright. It is the color of that *single terrifying phosphor-dot* recalled from the age of black and white TV. That dot the images *fell into* when the set was turned off. That very dot that lingered, sentient and utterly radioactive, in the dark.

And you . . .

You, the Preterite, are met, by night, in the aquamarine curvilinearity of the Drained Pools. (You offer us your hands.) We, the Elect (aspects, each, of the Kreator) dream of Babylon. We offer you, in passing, the glory of our Storm of Bronze.

Chickie rolls on.

Past North Beach Leather.

Past the white-boy bum, who's screaming, an empty bottle of Evian in either hand, "Hitler didn't lose, motherfucker; he just lacked the medium!"

Chickie blinks, gives his left-hand wheel a last, major shove, bounces off the curb, and plunges toward Santa Monica Boulevard, the Dot growing and just growing, the closer he gets.

1938 Ray Kreutzer, Pentecostal preacher and Dustbowl refugee, meets Miyoki Llewellyn at a revival meeting. They marry in Los Angeles.

1941 Anton Kreutzer born.

1944 Josie Kreutzer born. Miyoki sent to Manzanar internment camp.

1945 Miyoki contracts tuberculosis. Fatally. Onset of alcoholism and dementia in Kreutzer.

1945-57 Abuse and misery.

1957 Kreutzer Sr. dies. Josie sent to maternal grandparents in Japan.

1957-62 Tony Kreutzer's juvenile delinquency period.

1963 Kreutzer begins successful career as science fiction writer.

1966 Josie starts work at US consulate in Kyoto. Begins correspondence with Kreutzer viz. Japanese religion and philosophy.

1968 Kreutzer begins development of Synthiotics, a/k/a New Realism. Emergence of personality cult.

1969 Kreutzer meets visionary brain scientist Dex Wyckoff in northern California. Acid and late night discussions about the coming world mind.

1969-72 Kreutzer and Wyckoff start Mimecom Inc., to exploit Wyckoff's patents and pharmocological research.

1971 Start of Synthiotic street clinics. Kreutzer earns first

mainstream plaudits, begins New Realist penetration of government. Affair with Berenice Wyckoff commences.

1973 Harry Wyckoff born.

1974 Josie audits American History class of Prof. Eli Levitt. End of "arctic hysteric" period. Love, sexual obsession, and marriage.

1975 Successful experiments with brain implants and mental augmentation. Mimecom's future assured, despite untimely death of Wyckoff. Harry enters succession of New Realist foster homes.

1976 Grace born to Josie and Eli. Paige Katz also born.

1977 Synthesis of amazol, a pure entactogenic agent, based on Dex's research. Berenice enters clinic under supervision of Dr. Tobias Schenkl.

1978 Kreutzer forms Fathers. Divorce of Josie and Eli.

C H R O N

Eli returns to the U.S. Josie enters Buddhist monastery following mental breakdown. Beginning of Perceptories.

1979 Fathers begin campaign of vigilantism and childnapping. Kreutzer's various interests consolidated into Wild Palms Group. Eli remarries.

1980 Chickie Levitt born. Kreutzer enters politics, but Senate bid thwarted when Peter Katz exposes ties with Fathers.

Paige abducted and placed in Synthiotic foster home.

1981 Marriage of Josie and Masahiro Ito, a power in Japanese reality-industrial complex and business partner of Kreutzer.

1982 Mimecom starts farms for sub-rosa drug research.

1983 Business tensions between Kreutzer and Ito.

O L O G Y

Eli Levitt founds Friends to combat Kreutzer and Fathers. Harry becomes friends with Tommy Laszlo.

1984 Death of Ito. Controversial assumption of corporate control by Josie.

1986 "Satoriums" begin in Japan.

1988 Fathers murder Eli's second wife, cripple Chickie.

1989 Grace summers in Paris, becomes interested in fashion.

1991 Josie and Grace leave Japan for California. Wild Palms Group acquires Channel 3 TV network.

1992 Kreutzer begins affair with Paige Katz. Josie begins officially working with Wild Palms Group.

1993 Fathers' vigilantism and kidnappings stepped up. Harry Wyckoff and Paige Katz fall in love at UCLA.

1994 Kreutzer elected Senator. Trade war between US and Japan begins over digital TV. Harry enters law school.

1995 Grace and Harry elope. Josie estranged from Grace.

1996 Beginning of "Planned Depression." Birth of Coty Wyckoff.

1997 Boca Raton nuclear disaster (90,000 dead) results in unprecedented increase in police powers. Growth of

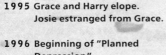

Fathers' political power. Campaign against Friends stepped up.

1998 Eli sentenced to Perceptory for putative role in Boca Raton. Chickie befriended by painter Tully Woiwode. Harry goes to work at Baum, Weiss, and Latimer. Chappie Starfall becomes first Synthiotic superstar.

1999 Fathers conclude successful campaign against Friends. Success of Schenkl's New Realism seminars.

2000 Ushio Kawabata and Chickie "meet" in web, start GO chip research.

2002 Depression ends. Rise of comedian Stitch Walken and actress Tabba Schwartzkopf.

2004 Deirdre Wyckoff born. Harry enters analysis with Dr. Schenkl.

2005 Chickie refines first practical virtual reality compression algorithm. Escalation of US trade war with Japan.

2006 Grace starts Vestiges boutique. Empathogenic research yields proto-mimezine.

2007 Mimecom announces next year's model: Mimecam. Mimecom Kyoto pirates Chickie's research to begin work on GO chip.

2008 Kreutzer announces Presidential candidacy. Premiere of "Church Windows." Start of black market in mimezine.

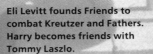

NOTES ON CONTRIBUTORS

ANA BARRADO is a photographer whose work has recently appeared in RE/SEARCH and ZONE, among other publications in the US and Japan. A monograph of her work was published in Tokyo by Atelier Peyotl.

PAT CADIGAN is the author of *Mindplayers*, *Synners*, and *Fools*. She messes up reality in Kansas.

FRED DEWEY is an essayist and screenwriter living in Los Angeles.

THOMAS DISCH's most recent novels are *The M.D.* and *The Businessman: A Tale of Terror* (Berkeley Books), coming out this summer.

RB DONNER is a Professor at London's School of Oriental and African Studies. The author of numerous monographs on Turkmeni and Pathan kinship systems, he is currently engaged in fieldwork outside of Islamabad.

ADAM DUBOV is a writer-director living in Los Angeles. Hopefully, with a little patience and a little luck, you'll be seeing one of his quality motion pictures soon at a theater near you.

JOHANN GEORG ECCARIUS was born May 12, 1818 in Erfurt, Thuringia, Germany. He is the author of two published novels, *The Last Days of Christ the Vampire* (1988) and *We Should Have Killed the King* (1990).

MARY GAITSKILL is the author of *Bad Behaviour*, a collection of short stories, and *Two Girls*, a novel.

WILLIAM GIBSON, who coined the word "cyberspace," is the author of *Neuromancer* and the forthcoming *Virtual Light*.

DR. GARY HENDERSON is a Professor of pharmacology and toxicology at UC Davis. He also coined the term "designer drugs."

MELISSA HOFFS is an artist living in Los Angeles.

JOHN HOMANS was until recently the Features editor of DETAILS magazine. He has recently assumed similar duties at the *New York Observer*.

E. HOWARD HUNT, a longtime CIA officer, is the author of seventy-five novels and two non-fiction works. His latest book is *Chinese Red*, published by St. Martin's Press.

NED JACKSON is a playwright living in New York City. He has been produced and published in the United States and Germany.

HILLARY JOHNSON is the author of the novel *Physical Culture*, about which the London Times said "This is the kind of book which could give sado-masochism a bad name." She lives in Los Angeles.

LEMMY KILMISTER is lead singer/bassist with well known hard rock band and surgical support demonstrators Motörhead. He is delighted. As often as possible.

BRENDA LAUREL got involved in the computer games business in 1976, and is now a senior researcher at Interval Research Corporation, from whence she is attempting to influence the future of human-computer interaction. She was also the science consultant on WILD PALMS.

JAMIE MALINOWSKI is the National Editor of *Spy* magazine. His novel, *Mr. Stupid Goes to Washington*, was published by Birch Lane in 1992.

SUEHIRO MARUO is perhaps the best-known and most extreme of the new generation of *manga* artists. Seven of his graphic novels have been published so far, and he recently had his first gallery show in Tokyo.

MALCOLM McLAREN is well-known as a clothing designer, impresario, and recording artist. He has lately been active as a producer of music, films, and television specials (which he also directs).

HANS MORAVEC has built and contemplated robots since childhood, obtaining a Stanford Ph.D. for a seeing robot that negotiated obstacle courses. He currently directs the Carnegie Mellon Mobile Robot Laboratory. His book *Mind Children*, and forthcoming others, discuss the eventual merger of machines and humanity.

NEUE SLOWENISCHE KUNST is an artists' collective based in Ljubljana, Slovenia, which encompasses the music group Laibach and the IRWIN group of painters. A monograph of their work was recently published by Amok Books.

GENESIS P. ORRIDGE has published essays on cultural engineering since 1964. He co-founded the Throbbing Gristle, Psychic TV and Coum Transmissions action collectives. As Transmedia (co-directed with Alaura P. Orridge), he collaborates on lectures with Timothy Leary and Hyperdelic Video throughout the US.

JANE PRATT is the founding editor of *Sassy* magazine, Editorial Director of *Dirt* magazine, host of the "Jane Pratt Show," and author of a book on American teenagers to be released next year.

HOWARD RODMAN's novel, *Destiny Express*, has also been published in England, France, Italy and Japan. As a screenwriter he has worked with Chantal Akerman, Robert Harmon, Errol Morris and Steven Soderbergh.

SPAIN RODRIGUEZ was creator of some of the first underground comics. He also recently designed stage sets and props for Ralph Bakshi's *Cool World*.

RALPH RUGOFF writes about vernacular museums, Pathetic Art and sewage treatment systems, and lives within shooting distance of a major freeway.

NORMAN SPINRAD is the author of about sixty stories and fifteen novels. He has written screenplays, film and literary criticism, and political commentary. His latest novel, *Russian Spring*, was published in 1991.

BRUCE STERLING is an author and journalist. His most recent book is *The Hacker Crackdown*.

BRUCE WAGNER is the author of *Force Majeure*, a novel.

PETER WOLLEN is a screenwriter and filmmaker who lives in London and Los Angeles. His new books, *Singing in the Rain* and *Raiding the Icebox*, are being published in 1993.

YASUSHI FUJIMOTO owns and runs CAP, a graphic design studio in Tokyo, from where he art-directs, among other projects, five magazines a month, including *Studio Voice* and the Japanese editions of *GQ* and *Marie-Claire*.

STUART SWEZEY is a founding editor and publisher of Amok Books.

ROGER TRILLING is currently the West Coast Editor of DETAILS magazine.